Disclaimer: The ideas and conclusions expressed in this work are the collection of my interpretation of my life's experiences and as such; one or more ideas may not meet your satisfaction. However, the purpose of this book is to convey a message and examine a highly incendiary plight common in society. The statement deadbeat dad remains a highly popularized term almost making those that bare it seems celebrated, pinning on them a badge of honor, when it should be a banner of shame. It is my hope that my work will convict society as a whole and force us to demand better for our posterity. Is that too much to ask, when we claim to love our children? I simply seek to present a social commentary on an all too common phenomenon, explore the roots of that problem and shed some guidance for those that have already and may someday find themselves in similar straits. I wish you much success and hope that I have done a great service to all that read this book.

This book, although based on true-life experiences, has been fictionalized and does not depict any actual person. Resemblance to any real people living or dead is absolutely coincidental. By virtue of the reader seeing this statement and continuing to read each ensuing page thereafter, you have provided your approval and have forfeited any right to petition this work.

Dedication

This book is dedicated to my mommy. She's a put all your business in the street while "giving honor to God/pray my strength in the Lord" testifying churchwoman whose familial interaction prepared a sister to write this baby-mama tell all. You know it took a special type of woman to be able to raise a child like Ms. KIA.

◆————————————◆

In life we have to learn to accept that friends & family will come and go along our journey. Sometimes we are blessed with someone who can celebrate and help you create your good times, who can talk you away from the edge, and then sit beside you on that edge...

Thank you Donna, RIH!!!

You have been a teacher, sister, sidekick and true & proven friend throughout the years!

There have been several times when I have thrown my hands up in frustration and wanted to quit but God blessed me with some great friends that keep me encouraged during the tough times...
Thank You...

Curtis, NJ- Mona, TX- Monica, NJ
Ms. Sorrell, TX - RIH

Table of Contents

FOREWORD

What you have in your hands is a most riveting tell-all of the personal struggle of a woman the likes of whom you will certainly find yourself drawn to immensely. Is this due to some surface impression -- could be, but if you are a person of substance, you will be probing deeper. It is here that the treasure of KIA Swain's dialogue makes her value palpable. KIA is and always has been a strong woman, but even knowing her as I do; I am taken back by the revelation of the tumultuous events that she experienced after we left college.

In all frankness, she and I enjoy a robust friendship that has survived its own share of blows, the heaviest of which scarred her and were caused by me. Just considering that in and of itself, speaks volumes to the great heart in this woman. For someone to not just accept the flaws in you, but to transcend the damage you have caused to them as a result of those flaws and continue to hold your hand in life, is an amazing show of courage, commitment and compassion.

During one of our routine phone conversations, Kia revealed to me that she had decided to write a book (this one) chronicling the story of her parentage. While so many were eager to show their resistance to her endeavor, I became her very own cheerleader. I had witnessed some of the obstacles she had been victorious in eradicating, so I already knew this would be an amazing story; however, I had no idea of its potential to place itself into the fabric of American society as an undeniable must-read.

This book will establish a multi-generational unification amongst people from all walks of life that are experiencing similar hardships.

She laughs when I say this, but I call it the single woman's guide to dealing with a deadbeat dad. It really is!

It's a rather perplexing occurrence in our society; we get ourselves into predicaments prior to acquiring proper knowledge and skill in handling these dilemmas.

KIA has the temerity to actually recognize this problem, relinquish her misgivings and provides an in-depth peek at the cause and effect (of being a single parent); to address the future need of individuals that will find themselves requiring this precious guidance.

Interestingly enough, this book isn't just for the ladies' entertainment. It's just as pertinent for men that want to gain insight into the plight of far too many women that suffer based on their trust and love for a man that doesn't deserve it: Men that abandon their off-spring as a method of chastising a woman that has matured and realized that what once was is no longer relevant for their happiness.

I know that KIA is thankful that you have chosen to read her work, but I hope that you will find yourself grateful that she was candid with such intimate knowledge. Please spread the word because we all know someone that needs this book. Hell, I did and yes I am in the book... yikes!

Prose, author of *Where is Love?*

Introduction

Family, relationships, and love are defined at home—our standards for them, our expectations from them, and our examples of them. As a young child, my mother was all I knew and was everything I wanted to be—until the day she welcomed my father back into our lives. I couldn't accept that she saw him as her children's father; I only saw the man who left us.

I spent my teen and young adult years despising women who required government assistance but who did not require the children's fathers to share responsibility for their children, other than buying the latest sneakers or giving them a couple of dollars here and there. Then the day came when I was faced with motherhood, and the one thing I hated, I became: a "baby mama." Faced with this reality, I had to do some soul-searching. Quite simply, I needed a fucking reality check.

I needed to stop lying to myself, to stop trying to hide from my true feelings and to take responsibility for my part in causing my problems.

I decided to try to be more than what was expected of me. I made a choice to face the pain of my past and to use it to fuel my passion for my future. But the reality of being a single mom autonomous of support from family and friends was scary and lonely enough to make me realize, that even the best game plan would only make baby steps toward my happily ever after. The healing process is long and sometimes lonely. The one thing that I learned is that, if you are an adult with issues with your mom or dad, you need to lie on somebody's couch and tell him or her all about them. But if you plan to *or* fuck up and become a parent, you can no longer use your unresolved issues with your mom or dad as the "poor me" rationale for not setting the example in your own children's lives and neglecting to be their provider.

Around 2003, I wrote a five-year plan for getting my life together. The plan included getting off state aid (Medicaid and welfare), graduating from a master's program, moving to Texas to become a teacher and writing a book. It's been an ordeal, and I have encountered a lot of pitfalls, but I never stopped wanting to write that book; I decided to focus on the audience of me, myself, and I.

This week has provided clear confirmation of the focus of my book. First, I attended the Essence Music Festival for free seminars, and I really enjoyed the overall setup. The speakers were the best in the business, and even though I didn't agree with all the messages, I did respect the different points of view. The concept of the Essence Party with a Purpose was wonderful.

It felt great to be able to attend a popular event that offered knowledge, networking, and personal empowerment information, even at a point in my life when I didn't have the financial means to even buy a fountain drink from the snack bar.

One would probably think I am financially set or that I am bourgeois, and though I have attained numerous degrees and accolades, this book is not about statistics for my educated colleagues or for the self-righteous, religious community; It's about trying to turn the pain of my past into absolute passion for my future. We always consider that someone's story has a beautiful or bitter beginning, but people tend to jump straight to the "Happily Ever After" ending. Baby Mama Memoirs recounts the miserable middle and chronicles my pursuit to define and secure my own "Happily Ever After".

Childhood of a Future Baby Mama

Train up a child in the way he should go,

And when he is old he will not depart from it."

–Proverbs 22:6 NJKV

My Own Memoirs...

Before you began to read the following section of this book I would like to challenge you review the questions below and get your **Mind Set** for the section...

1. What was you family structure as a child? (eg. Mom, Dad, Sibling, etc)
   a. _____
   _____
   _____

2. Who was the main provider (s) for family as a child?
   a. _____
   _____

3. Did you have any questions as a child that was avoided by adult s or never addressed?
   a. _____
   _____
   _____

4. Choose five adjectives to describe you father...
   a. _____
   b. _____
   c. _____
   d. _____
   e. _____

5. What is most important lesson your father taught you that helps you in your adult years?
   a. _____
   _____
   _____

Daddy's Deathbed

November 2008

My brother called to inform me that our dad was in the hospital for the past couple of days because of an inability to have a bowel movement. He said the doctors needed to run several tests to figure out what was going on. This call made me reflect on a question that I had been asking myself for years: "How can a man make a baby and leave it (during the child's growing years) and then make peace with God and enjoy the benefits of good ole Heaven?"

Simply put, my question was "Do deadbeat dads go to heaven?"

My father was diagnosed with an advanced stage of colon cancer, and my aunt urged me to change my scheduled Christmas vacation and come to New Jersey immediately, if I wanted to see him alive. I replied, "He better stick around till Christmas, or I'll see you all at the funeral." A week later he died.

As I sat in the front row of my daddy's funeral at his "going home" service, speaker after speaker and preacher after preacher praised the great deeds of my dad. I sat thinking to myself that all this time I'd been thinking that he never knew me, and I realized that it went both ways, because I damn sure didn't know the man they were talking about.

Hell, at the family viewing the night before, I had been in the waiting area of the church when a group of women ushers and church sisters asked how I knew Deacon Swain.

"I'm supposed to be his youngest kid," I said.

To my surprise, they said, "We knew that was you. Deacon Swain talked about you so much we already knew you and your boys as soon as you all walked in."

"Who, me?" I asked. "Are you sure you're talking about me?"

Then I proceeded to walk back into the church and take my seat, socializing with family members I had not seen in over ten years.

It took twenty-eight years of me asking, "Why don't I have a daddy" but like most questions, the answer came from finding peace within. And just when I thought I had come to terms with my issues with my dad, there I was reliving this shit over with my kids.

Single Mama Survival Skills

People kill me when they tell "As a child, we were so poor" stories. Most kids don't know anything about their situations, especially when the situation is common in their environment. In my family and neighborhood, some people had a little more than others or dressed a little bit better, but in the end, living in the low-income apartments was the local cool hangout spot. Most drug dealers and other "man-children" lived with their mothers or baby mamas, and being poor didn't stop someone's popularity.

My mother raised my brothers and me in a four-bedroom, one-and-a-half bathroom apartment in a low-income housing complex. We were really a family unit; we color-coordinated our clothes every Sunday for church, and everywhere we went was a family outing, from the school's open house to grocery shopping. For years, my mother didn't have a car, so we walked everywhere, and free school lunch was just a given.

I just thought my mother was old-fashioned, and it wasn't until I went to college that I came to understand that we were financially challenged (more like poor as hell).

That was why we shopped in thrift stores for our first-day-of-school outfits, why we wore handmade clothes, picked out of donation boxes in public parking lots, and why we ate raw hot dogs for lunch when we went to the boardwalk. I learned a lot of money management skills because of my mother's survival tactics, which she used for providing a stable home environment via government funding.

During my childhood, my only real connection with my father was my aunt Rose and her eight or so children who happened to live two doors over in the same low-income housing development I grew up in. My close relationship with my aunt Rose was the only real connection, or should I say *proof*, that my father even existed.

Daddy's Little Girl

I always wondered what my father looked like. I know that sounds cliché, but I just figured that, because I didn't have the style or look of my cousins on my father's side of the family (they were well dressed and groomed with light skin and wavy hair), maybe that was why he didn't want to be around me. It's not hard for a child to think that way, especially when her daddy doesn't call her (with the exception of Father's Day) and never comes to see her. If the adults never explain why, she thinks it must be because of something she did or something that he doesn't like about her.

I hear many single mothers proudly announce how they refuse to say anything ill or negative about the absent father, but I believe that it has more to do with that woman protecting her feelings, more than her child's. Perhaps this isn't so in your case; in mine, an ex-boyfriend and later the baby daddies saying they HATED me, I was CRAZY, or that I wasn't SHIT and FUCK me was something I really did want to talk about or deal with.

These men weren't one-night stands and I wasn't their jump-off. I dated these men; we stayed under the same roof, we knew each other's family & friends. I damn sure didn't know how they could think it was okay to simply walk out of my life; how could I explain that to my child? Saying nothing has no nobility, but you do it because you sometimes just don't know what to say; you're dealing with revealing your abandonment issues, which leaves you nerveless to address your child's curiosity.

The only story my aunts (my mother's sisters) told was of the time my mom and dad were having one of their many fights and he couldn't get to my mom. In his frustration, he picked up my baby swing and threw it into the wall across the room with me in it! They told me that I didn't even cry or fall out of the swing. *Damn... that's a fucked-up story to know about your father.*

There were no pictures of him holding me on the day of my birth or of him standing behind me at my first birthday party or of him knocked out asleep on the couch with me in his arms.

My only recollection of his silhouette is from one day

when my mom and I were standing on the corner of Fourth Street in front of a big white building. I was kneeling down and playing in the mud with my yellow teakettle, and my mom started talking to this mean man. I filled up my yellow teakettle with wet mud and threw it all over the man's white suit. Before I could look up at the man to stick my tongue out, my mother grabbed me: the man just turned and walked away.

When I mentioned that story to my mother during my adolescent years, she informed me that the man was my father, and she had been arguing with him. She said she remembered it well, because she thought he was going to kill me for getting his new white-on-white suit dirty.

Favorite Day of the Year

My daddy was JoJo Swain; that's what everyone called him. A fatherly presence or a mere image was unheard of in our home with the exception of his faithful call once a year on Father's Day to be wished a happy Father's Day from his bastard children. I can't remember the exact age, but I believe it was when I was about seven or eight when the daddy drama started. Every year, I would get slapped or whipped for refusing to wish my deadbeat dad a Happy Father's Day. The reason behind my anger was because, one Father's Day, he promised he would send me a scooter and get me a canopy bed for my upcoming birthday.

As any other child would do, I went and bragged to all of the other kids, especially Mona. She told me that I didn't have a daddy because no one had ever seen him and he didn't come to pick me up like her daddy did.

Mona lived with her grandmother, but she had 100 percent of attention from both her single mother and her father & his mother, who faithfully picked her up every weekend. August 16th came and went, and I felt so ashamed and stupid for even believing the words of a man I couldn't even remember seeing; more disdainfully, the stranger that only contacted us on his day (Father's Day) and not on my birthday.

On the next Father's Day, when it was my turn to talk to him, I told him that he was a liar; pointed out that he never called on Christmas or on our birthdays and told him I hated him. My mother quickly grabbed me off the phone and whipped my ass. Every year after that, I proudly took my slap or two for refusing to wish my dear old daddy a Happy Father's Day. Out of sight, out of mind, Daddy.

Walk Away & Don't Look Back Baby

My first real memory of a baby mama would have to be of my Aunt Addison (my mother's baby sister). Aunt Addie never came over to our apartment, but one school day right after she had just had a baby, I caught a glimpse of her walking up to the apartment. I was six years old, and I know this because her daughter and I are six years apart. I rushed out to meet her with the baby, and we walked to the steps of my apartment, where she sat down and started looking for something. My mom was in the kitchen, and she came to the screen door and offered Aunt Addie something to eat, but my aunt refused and just sat there looking for something. Later, my aunt asked me if I could tell time. I lied and said yes, so she sent me in to check the time. I asked my mom for the time and reported back to my aunt.

After what seemed like hours of us just sitting & looking and as it began to get dark, she just stood up and went over to the porch of her classmate's apartment to show her daughter off. Then she just walked away like whatever she was looking for didn't matter anymore.

As an adult, I can reflect back on my aunt just walking away from a man who didn't want to be bothered by their baby, and I can admire her strength and pride. But as you'll read later on in this book, I'm no Aunt Addison, and even as a child, I didn't mind starting some shit with a baby daddy.

I can't recall when or where I heard it or who said what, but it was known that my Aunt Addison (my mother's baby sister) had a baby with the son of Aunt Rose (my father's sister); he was my cousin and lived two apartments down from us. My cousin wasn't around much, because he was "the smart one" who was away in college, and then he moved out of the state when he graduated. Well, in the meantime, I always had a special connection with my little cousin; maybe it was because she had something I was curious about—a father—and I knew him.

After the day my aunt walked away with the baby, I

couldn't remember a time when she brought the baby over. Of Course, being a little busybody, nosey-ass, sassy-talking kid, I made it my duty to know every time my cousin was coming into town.

I also made sure that my 11-year-old ass would find a way to get my cousin from across town to my apartment so she could see her father. That shit got old quick, and one day he made it clear that he wasn't fucking with her. The shit he pulled and how he went about it, helped lay the foundation for my hatred of deadbeat dads. My little cousin Aana and I still talk about that day, because we both remember it all too well.

This is crazy as hell, because my college-educated cousin had gotten married and had two kids who were toddlers at the time. Of course, I overheard them planning to take the kids down the street to the park, and I eagerly asked if my little cousin was invited to go too. My male cousin responded "Oh, yeah," so I rushed her back to my apartment so I could put Aana in a cute outfit and fix her hair.

We used the upstairs bathroom so I could get her ready while we watched out the window to make sure we weren't going to miss them. Damn, we were both happy as hell that she was going with her daddy. The phone rang, and I picked up. I can't remember if it was Aunt Rose or my cousin's wife, but she said, "The car will be too crowded, so they will get her next time." Standing right next to me, my little cousin heard the same thing.

Since we were still in the upstairs bathroom, we looked out the window and waited to see her father, his wife, and just their two toddlers get in their yellow station wagon to go to the park. The tears just started rolling from her eyes, and even though she didn't make a sound, the sadness on her face made us both realize that she didn't have a daddy either.

I was so confused. I couldn't understand why Aana didn't have a father. You see, I was a funny-looking little girl, and I heard my father was a drunk who couldn't even read. However, Aana was a pretty little girl, and her father was smart and had gone to college. Why didn't he like her?

I felt like a real fucked-up because it was my fault that she was hurt. Her mother never brought her around, and no one on her father's side had ever taken the initiative to request her presence, but I brought her over there, and because of that, she was hurt by the truth.

You don't have to read the last chapter to know what happened next. My little cousin is married. She became a successful business owner and recently became a mother. She personally invited her "daddy", who lives fifteen minutes away, to be part of her special moments. I supported her choice to reach out to him, but I didn't agree that she should be the one trying to reach out. I understood she wanted to believe that he could change or that she could get closure for herself.

Deep inside, the little girl in me wanted to believe he would come to her wedding, but you already know... he never came out the door that day and never look back for the baby he left behind. I told her, "Memories have been and will continue to be made with or without his ass!"

Love at First Sight

I was twelve years old when my Aunt Rose told me that my daddy was coming to town. I acted as though I didn't care, but I was really excited to meet my dad. I wondered what he looked like, what he would say to me, and if he would have all the things he had promised me all those years before.

It was a Sunday when Aunt Rose called and said, "Your father is here." I was so excited that I rushed over to finally meet him. When I barged in through the door as I usually did, my cousin Dee called out to JoJo that I was there, but I didn't see any new faces appear. They called out to him again, and still I saw no new face. Finally, someone said he was standing in the bathroom, so I walked over to the open door, and there was this black-ass, frowning face looking down at me. There was no greeting hug, no "I missed you" kiss on the forehead, not a word—just a disdainful glare.

The moment became so awkward that all I could wonder was that, whatever I looked like at that moment—whether it was my hair, my skin, my smile, or my clothes—was too much for him to show me any type of affection or love.

I broke the silence by asking in my smart-ass tone, "So do you have any money for us?" "No," he said, and I turned away and went back to my house to get away from the tense situation.

Deadbeat Grandmas Do's & Don'ts

True to the nature of a nosey project busybody, as soon as I laid my little cousin Aana's bullshit to rest, I was off stirring up shit somewhere else. Word on the street was that my oldest brother had a baby with one of the Brown sisters. One day, I was at summer camp, and one of the sisters was working there with her little daughter, so I just went over and asked if that was my brother's baby. Mind you that I was just about thirteen years old and talking to a grown woman.

She cursed my ass out saying, "Ain't nobody fucked or want no damn Omar ass. I don't know what the fuck you heard!" When she finished her rant, she went on to invite me to her apartment the next time I was in her building complex if I really wanted to know more about my brother real child. I made it my business to get there, and as I stood in her living room she proceeded to her coffee table and picked up an eight-by-ten framed picture of a little boy with cornrows. "This is your nephew," she said.

"He's down south, but they are moving back here soon."

I went home and told my mother that Omar had a kid. She just looked at me and we left it at that. Omar was the oldest of all my many brothers and he was exactly twenty years older than me. He'd already had three kids by two ex-wives by that time, and that's all we had known about, and he wasn't actively involved in their lives outside of child support orders. Ironically, he was in a long-term relationship with another lady and gladly providing time and support for her three preteen and teenage kids.

The following summer there was a knock at the door. I met my mother at the door, and there was a lady who looked like one of the fly girls from In Living Color and the cute little boy from the picture. I could tell my mother was familiar with the girl, but the girl was still nervous as she delivered a speech.

That speech went something like this: "I just want you to know that you have a grandson. We had a test and everything, and I don't want nothing from you all. I just want him to know his other family. He loves going to church." As my mother was a "holier than thou" church-going woman, she just nodded her head in approval and smiled, and then Shay and her son left. The next day or so I came into the house and heard Omar ranting to my mother. "FUCK THAT BITCH," he yelled. "She's a whore who just wants my money."

I decided to put my two cents in and said, "Well, she said you all took a test to prove the boy is your son.

"Now that was the ultimate betrayal. How dare I focus on the child? I was supposed to automatically side with my brother, even if he was doing a child wrong. Omar stormed out of the house, and I turned to my mother.

"What are you going to do about Omar and the baby?" I asked. "That's for Omar to decide, and if he don't want to get into that, I'm not going to get in that," she said. "That's your son. You can make him take care of his child," I said. "I can't make a grown man do anything," she said. I replied "That grown man is your child...You're still his mother, and that means something. If he's not going to step up, you should; At least spend time with the boy and take him to church with you." My mother never took him to church! I

I Declare War

There was never anything special between my father and me. I couldn't help Aana have any special moments with her father. Now there was a little boy looking for the same thing, and I was on the fucked-up father's side. **I declared war!**

My entire family was comprised of single mothers, baby mamas, and mother-child scenarios, but no one sympathized with Shay and her child. My brother was downright nasty to Shay. He went out his way to show his disgust towards his own son, and my entire family cosigned onto his bullshit behavior by not saying anything or stepping up and treating the innocent child like a family member. Hell no, that shit was wrong as hell. The boy was so beautiful, and I'm not just talking about his features though he was a cutie too. He was just curious about a part of himself that he knew nothing about. There was no way I was going to let my bitch-ass brother determine the importance of this child; so I made him my world and brought him into our family's world (which wasn't much, just a whole bunch of broke-ass people, like most of the families in my community). I would get him every weekend when I didn't have a track meet, and at first, my brother tried everything to humiliate Shay and her son Quan.

One day when Quan was with me at my mom's apartment, a teary-eyed Shay sped into the parking lot. She jumped out of her truck, yelling, "Go get my damn child, 'cause he don't have to come over here." I asked her what was up, and she told me that my brother had seen her at the community center and started cursing her out in front of everybody about bringing her child to his mother's house, so she was coming to get her child. I informed her that he didn't run anything and that my nephew was with his aunt. I said I would gladly let Omar know that he might not be a father, but I was an aunt. With that, Shay left, my nephew stayed with me, and my bitch-ass brother didn't come over to talk that shit to me. **The war was on.**

A few weeks later, Quan and I were walking through the parking lot back to my house. Omar, his girlfriend, and my mother were standing on the sidewalk. As we walked by, Quan said, "Hi, Omar."

"What the fuck you talking to me for?" my brother responded.

I fired first. I pushed my nephew to the side and stepped over to my brother, saying, "You better never talk to him. What kind of man ...blah blah..." I started. Then I called his girlfriend and my mother out for just standing there like they were okay with the bullshit he had just pulled.

A week later, my brother came in my room to offer twenty-five dollars to get Quan something for his birthday. I declined the cash and told him that I didn't run a closed-door kid charity.

Shay went on with her life and I remained a welcomed member of their family unit. However, no matter how much time I tried to spend with Quan, I assume it still didn't allay the impact of realizing the certainty that his daddy was a deadbeat.

As he got older and was really able to try to reach out to his sperm donor, he had to negate my position in his life. I even heard that he referred to me as being "a big mouth" or as someone who "talked too much," in an effort to show his loyalty to his sperm donor. At first it hurt to hear that was how he felt about me, but then I had to remind myself that **I had declared war** because I wanted to prove to him and to my family that this child was worth it to me and it was my job to show him.

Fast-forward twenty years later, and sorry to say, my nephew and I have grown apart. He is a father now, and I hope that nurture will outweigh nature.

A Woman's Worth in the Hood

By this time in my life, I had clearly learned about two types of women in my neighborhood: the woman who just got her ass beaten and the woman who beats ass. The most distinct memory of the bitch that gets her ass beaten would have to be of my cousin's girlfriend, Tanya. Tanya was a nineteen-year-old teen mother of a two-year-old, so when she hooked up with my cousin, of course she had to have a baby by him (who was about four months old by then).

As usual, they would have routine fistfights, but one time it got really wild in the parking lot. This was a special fight, because Tanya ran up to him with a metal bat. My cousin grabbed it from her, and began to hit her in her ass and legs to make her dance for the surrounding crowd to laugh. However, when the police finally arrived, the bat disappeared and the crowd didn't know anything. To make matters worse, Tanya wanted to talk shit and show her ass in front of the cops.

As she was being escorted from my aunt Rosa's

apartment with her kids, she started yelling, "I don't want your fucking baby. I'll throw her ass in the trash." Well that did it; her ass was arrested. To avoid the Department of Human Services being called to take her two baby girls, I willingly volunteered my busybody thirteen-year-old ass to take the girls to my house next-door. The next day, I didn't attend school and didn't hear anything from Tanya, who was rumored to have been released early that morning. In the late evening, I barged into my aunt's house to find Tanya sitting on my cousin's lap, kissing him and saying how much she loved him. I rushed back to my house and brought her damn kids to her. I remember thinking she was the stupidest bitch ever. How could she kiss and say she loved a man who had just beaten her with a bat for public entertainment, gotten her arrested, and didn't care where the kids went? How could she walk past my house where her kids were, to spend time with him? Stupid bitch!

Ah, but then there was Aunt Rose, of whom I spoke earlier.

She had eight mostly grown kids, and even though she lived as a single woman, she was married. I know, because every Friday, I would faithfully ride with her to go get her money from her husband.

One early Saturday morning as I walked over to my aunt's house to eat, I met my uncle rushing out the door. Out of nowhere, my aunt flew off her two-step porch right behind him and landed with a roundhouse punch to the side of his face. It took three of my aunt's full-grown sons—all over six feet tall—to pull her off of him, and she didn't stop beating her husband up until she was tired.

I was in awe. Damn, my aunt wasn't playing any games. She wasn't putting on a show. She was in it to simply fuck his ass up, and she did. I'm not going to lie; I loved what I saw. Hell, most of the time in my neighborhood, it was a woman getting her ass beaten, getting slapped around, or just acting stupid, but not this time. From that moment, my aunt was the standard of what type of woman from the hood I wanted to be if I was ever in that situation.

Words of Wisdom

Antonio was my first boyfriend, and we dated for eleven months. When I first started dating Antonio, he had long hair, he smoked, hung on the block, and even though he worked, you would classify him as a "street thug". Hell, I liked him, and my mother didn't. Out of nowhere he found Christ and got "Saved" and filled with the "Holy Ghost"; at least, that was the excuse he used to go and pray for his ex-girlfriend at her apartment at nine at night.

 I was about to really fuck his car up when my cousin Flav (who just happened to be chilling on the block at that time) pulled me to the side. "You can't do shit about what he is doing," he said, "So why make yourself look like an ass going to jail? Just stop fucking with him."

Being the Leo that I am, I couldn't let it ride, so the low-income housing drama queen in me went home and got about seven tubes of my dollar beauty supply lipstick and left a "caught-your-bitch-ass" note over all his windows.

A note for crazy chicks who don't want to go to jail for property damage, one-dollar lipstick is the hardest thing to get off of car windows.

Sometime after his prayer session, he discovered my lovely letter and came to my house to find my friend and me sitting on the trunk of her car. He demanded that I clean his car right away. I responded with a laugh, and he replied with the famous "bitch" label. The shock came when I saw my holier-than-thou Mother standing in the doorway just watching.

"Mom, you see how your son in Christ is talking to me?" I called out to her. She turned and walked back into the house without saying a word. As often as my mother jumped up in the name of Jesus against any wrongdoing, she wasn't going to say anything to this man cursing her baby daughter out at our own house.

He stood there mad as hell for a moment, like he wanted to do something, so I happily informed him that, if I got up to clean those windows, he wasn't going to have any damn car windows.I don't know if he took his mad ass on home, but I know he got the fuck out of my face.

No one else knew the whole story except my friend Sheren who was with me that night, but the next day, I came home from school to my mother and JoJo sitting in the kitchen. As soon I got completely in the door, JoJo said, "Antonio is a good young man, and you shouldn't leave him just because he beats you. You need to get hit in that mouth of yours!"

My mother said something under her breath, and I didn't wait to hear it. "You got me fucked up, nigga," I told him. "You might whip her ass," I pointed at my mother. "But I'm not taking no beating in the name of some bullshit love." Then I proceeded to go my room and let them stew over that.

I didn't get back together with Antonio, but it was because I found out he had a seven-year-old son in the Carolinas and a three-year-old across town whom he wasn't actively involved with, and I didn't want to deal with or be a part of another fatherless child's story. I didn't stick around to see how that story would end, but my brother recently saw Antonio and reported that he was still doing the church thing and was a happily married family man. "And why the fuck are you telling me?" I asked.

A College Girl Good Life

I went off to college single and sexy. My father's disdainful glare that day in the bathroom had built a foundation that I reconfigured to add to my own sexually independent allure. The fraternity boys, the football stars, the thugs and even the preppies couldn't understand why I wasn't seeking their approval or attention. I wasn't trying to be someone's girlfriend, wife, or baby-mama. College was the start of what I thought was my bright beginnings; my aggressive and independent mannerisms kept a vast majority of new college peers at bay. The new, college Ms. KIA was an extrovert with a busy school life (fifteen credits, cross-country, track, volunteering, daily library sessions, student clubs, work-study jobs, waitressing and college parties).

However, when I returned home the new me became yet a different me. I became an introvert because I understood that about 98% of my family and community were not there to be supportive or didn't think, desire or even believe that I could accomplish my educational endeavor; so I was sure to keep the school shit at school. Even though I wasn't the 4.0 students, I strived to be, I still won numerous rewards and recognitions for my grades and participation which was only a big deal to me, myself, and I.

Cyrus formally introduced himself in the first few weeks of school, during our freshman year. As he stood at my dorm door holding a football, he asked, "If someone liked you what would they have to do to get with you?" "It all depends on what type of game they have," I replied. "What if they don't have no game," Cy said. With my sinister smirk on my face I proceeded to walk over, stand directly in front on his huge, football-playing ass and tell him, "Everyone has game, baby". Cyrus got the hell out of my dorm room and face quick as hell.

Like most dudes who have the heart to make it through two conversations with me, Cy and I became great friends. For example, between his extra-large frame and my greedy ass, we would both be hungry as hell, and we would still split our one sub and share with each other.

At the beginning of sophomore year I was called upon to come to the apartments at two o'clock (in the morning) to meet with governing members of a popular fraternity & sorority. I guess they had a problem with something I had said and wanted me to clear it up. Cy and a member of the frat from my hometown, walked with me.

We walked in and the discussion ensued. During the heated dialogue, one of the girls attempted to rush me and instinctively, I attempted to knock her head off. She went off into a rant about how she was with all of her frat family and I was the bitch that was alone. I responded, "Well one of y'all in here is going to get really fucked up", but truth be told, I knew my boy Cy was there, so I wasn't too worried. Then I posed a question that required Cy to show his true colors and to my shock, he threw my ass under the bus. The moment he betrayed me, all my focus jumped from the frat family and with tears streaming from my eyes, I focused all my anger and hurt on his ass. The night ended with Cyrus choosing the frat over my friendship and that frat family never making the mistake of entreating my ass again. People hanging you out to dry were an all too familiar common, characteristic back at home;

that's why I always rolled solo. As a result of Cy's betrayal, he made himself dead to me and I returned to business as usual.

School life was great: as I stated earlier, I received a scholarship, numerous awards for my grades, partied my ass off, was cast in a play, worked campus jobs, volunteered, developed some great "friends with benefits", and still managed to maintain good grades, even without having the several hundred dollars necessary for my books (for two semesters). Most people back at home would have sworn I was down south somewhere because I never went back home with the few exceptions of my little cousin Aana calling about girls jumping in her face; then I would take the hour and a half drive to go and beat a bitch's ass and zip right back to school, to my studies.

To deal with the stress and anxiety of surviving school, I became a devoted runner and did some hard partying and enticing dances. I stayed away from three things: "I love you," relationships, and men with kids. Ironically, during my senior year, I broke my own damn rules and tried all three at one time.

With the end of my undergrad college journey approaching, I was on track; I had completed all the necessary work for graduation minus one general introductory class. I had already qualified to apply to graduate in December, which meant I would have finished my four year degree in three and half years. Right before the start of the fall semester, Cyrus returned from his oversees student exchange and as I walked out the Morrison Hall office, he stepped directly into my path and asked if we could please talk for a moment. I agreed and he proceeded to apologize about that night two years ago. I accepted his apology, but I lived by the philosophy that "Sorry don't fix shit." Cy went a step farther though, wanting to prove that he could make it up to me.

Even though I didn't have any hoops for him to jump through, he started making his own hoops to show his sincerity. Appreciating his effort, I said the hell with it; if all else fails I would at least get in enough time to "hit it."

I realized I hadn't spoken to him in two years, but I was very aware of the rumor that he was laying out some great dick. I had never been big on the relationship thing, but he spoiled the mess out of me; I mean before anything could become an issue, he had already resolved it. It felt really nice to finally let my guard down, but before I knew it, we were once again faced with him having to show me his loyalty. This time it was with nasty "Yuk Butt" whore trying to play that "We Just Real Good Friends " bullshit. Again he betrayed me.

The official seven-week relationship was a horrible train wreck that almost cost me everything I had worked for during my college years; it brought out the raw beast in me. I didn't like the way I felt. Knowing what I was capable of (fucking a nigga up) was something I didn't want to deal with.

Court date after court date, getting kicked off campus, thugs at home acting like assholes because I didn't want them outside of the hood— it was just too much to deal with. The Cyrus relationship proved that something was terribly wrong and it had to be me, because the hurt and abandonment I felt at home, I now felt in college from the person I chose to have in my life.

When the dust settled and I was free to go, I ran like Forrest Gump. I didn't have a purpose or a plan, I just ran, because I didn't want to go back and deal with the pain of my past. With no plan, preparation, or sense of purpose, I packed my Mitsubishi Eclipse and drove out of New Jersey. I drove south with tears streaming down my face and bopping to my Newark club music. The long drive ended with me in the dirty south, staying at one relative's house or the other's still with no plan, preparation, or sense of purpose

Living the Generational Curse

So you're having my baby
And it means so much to me
There's nothing more precious
Than to raise a family

−Jodeci, "Forever My Lady"

My Own Memoirs...

Before you began to read the following section of this book I would like to challenge you review the questions below and get your **Mind Set** for the section...

1. Describe your idea family structure...

   a. _____
   _____
   _____

2. Who is apart of your family support system? (Present family or during your childhood ... eg. grandma)

   a. _____
   _____
   _____

3. Would you have or advise someone on having a child knowingly that father dose not want a relationship with the mother and unborn child?

   a. _____
   _____
   _____

4. Do you know someone who has feeling on distain for a child and why?

   a. _____
   _____
   _____

5. Does a parent dependant on government assistances (eg. Food stamps, Section 8/Income housing) realistically have anything to offer their children?

   a. _____
   _____
   _____

Show What You Know

'm not supposed to say this, because I'm an educator and I consider myself to be a lifelong learner, but at that point in my life and many more to follow, I felt really deceived and cheated by the results of my investment in the educational accomplishment of attaining a college degree. As a first-generation college student, coupled with my family's socioeconomic status and my minority classification, I was accepted to a state college through an equal opportunity funding program.

This program allowed underprivileged and otherwise forgotten students an opportunity to get their foot into college doors. With my lack of a family support system, a label of being learning-disabled, and low SAT scores (760), this was my only way to attempt a four-year postsecondary education.

Once I got there, I loved campus college life—living in the dorms, being in student clubs, participating in team sports, going to Greek parties—but academically, I had to play catch-up quick if I was going to stay and be successful. I expended enormous time and effort to attain that degree, but I did not understand how to translate my school knowledge into a career after graduation. I thought that simply having the paper degree would guarantee me vast job opportunities, because that was what society had advertised and the school fallaciously perpetuated.

After about four months of no callbacks, no real place to stay to get off my feet, and only being able to secure work at the local Popeyes as an hourly cashier, I just decided to show what I knew.

I didn't plan on having a baby, but I damn sure didn't protect myself from making a kid either. I said that dumb bullshit that most dumb ass girls say: *"Well, if God lets me get pregnant, then he must want me to have a child."*

I'm ashamed as hell as I type this sentence, but it's what I told myself to justify my bullshit.

Just think about how people make *their* fucked up choices and avoid taking responsibility for *their* part in *their* own problems. We blame others—the devil and God—when it was simply our own foolish selves doing   some   dumb   shit.

Shut Up!

SHUT UP, SHUT UP, SHUT THE FUCK UP!

I don't want to hear you saying that I'm not the first baby mama and I won't be the last, that things will work out in time, or that I should give it to God. Hell, every day, I was crying my eyes out, begging God to take the pain away. All I felt was pain, hurt, and shame. It's not supposed be like this; men shouldn't just walk away from their children. How the hell could I have been naive enough to lay with such an asshole: one that would walk out on his flesh and blood just to hurt me? Most single mothers don't consider sharing the mundane details of the daily struggles of rearing a child alone: they simply accept it as their role. When they do address parenting, they tend to give a very vague description with a suck-it-up-and-move-on attitude.

All I could think about was how I was going to tell my child he didn't have a father because of me.

Welcome to the Dumb-Dumb Club

Raise your right hand—hell, throw both hands up to the sky—and repeat after me:

"My name is [your full name] and all in the name of a dick (or clit), I did some dumb-ass shit."

If flashbacks just went through your mind of some shit you did, but can't say out loud, you may be an official member of a very peculiar group: If not, perhaps you haven't been in the game long enough ... but just stick around. Most members can tell a personal story of love, lies, and the life after. The depth of the situation determines one's membership level in this fraternal order. The intake process happens when one person willingly interacts with their ignorant partner. During the course of this relationship, that person willingly does things that don't make any fucking sense: justifying his or her bullshit in the name of love, and proudly holding their head up to live the lie. With that, she/he has crossed the sands and become an honored neophyte of the secret society the Dumb-Dumb Club.

Unfortunately, most get their membership during their teens and young adult years. During that time, they had hoped to learn their lessons about love, lies, and life: to use that knowledge to become self-aware and a better person. However, the many that refuse to live, love, and learn are classified as active members and create the criterion of the Dumb-Dumb Club.

Examples include but are not limited to the baby mama claiming to have years in a relationship with the baby daddy and there still isn't a Wal-Mart family portrait in her possession; Dating a married man and bragging about how your two to three hours each week are his special moments; You're not in a committed relationship but your man has a key to come and go as he pleases. He drives your car around town while you're at work; you're engaged wearing a ring you bought your damn self. You glamorize struggling to raise your four or five kids and the only reason you won't have your tubes tied is because of your hopes that the next baby daddy will be your claim to fame; bragging about having a man or boo even though Uncle Sam is the one providing the family's food, shelter, and medical care every month and you still have the nerve to lay with that man or boo every night—hell, the only people who know about the relationship are his boys and his male family members.

I am the single mother of two, and I must admit that I didn't get my official lifetime membership into the Dumb-Dumb Club until my second child. During my first pregnancy, I received my official "Crazy as Hell" card, which was just my pre-pledge process for the lifetime membership, which I would receive in the near future.

Becoming a VIP lifetime member requires more than acting like a fool over some good sex; I had to pay a hefty price financially and emotionally both publicly and privately. It took every fiber of my being to struggle out of that shit to reach my VIP club status.

The only plus side is that I didn't have to be an active member to use my "I'll Pass on Your Sorry Ass" card. Baby Mama Memoirs tells of the madness— how I felt and dealt with others while trying to adjust to my role as a new mother.

99.9 Percent

There's a 99.9 percent chance that if the father doesn't give a fuck about that baby in the womb, he's not going to be bothered for the next eighteen years or longer. The first time I was told this, I was six months pregnant and walking from one of my cousin's house. A very popular nosey older woman was sitting on her porch. She beckoned for me to come to her as I walked past her house. I really didn't care for the smart-mouthed old woman, but out of traditional norms of dealing with elders, I stopped and entertained her for a minute.

After the nosey, bold woman asked me how I was doing, she cut straight to the point and said, "You're a little firecracker, so what are you trying to prove with all that fighting and stuff?"

"I'll prove my shit with a DNA test, and that will be all she wrote," I said in response.
"I've known that boy since he was a baby and seen many more like him," she said, "and a test won't make that boy into a father."

I ignored that and said, "Okay, I got to go."

I Fucked Him Up, and It Felt Good

I had just found out that I was about six weeks pregnant when Raheem aka "Radio Raheem" and I had a very cordial discussion about the pregnancy, as we had already ended our relationship a few weeks earlier. During that conversation, he informed me that he had just started dating a new girl about two weeks prior but that he would end it to get back together in the hopes of marriage once the baby was born. His brisk offer of a happily ever after and the story about his new girlfriend of two weeks seemed a bit contrived, so I suggested that we simply work on building a stronger friendship if we planned on being parents. In what seemed like an overnight transformation, my ex became a straight-up asshole. I guess after he had time to discuss the pregnancy with his family and friends, he realized that he was sterile and girls just wanted him for his hood riches. He wanting a DNA test didn't shock me. I personally believe that everyone should get one—but his new nasty attitude in public had me feeling incensed, and my anger started to grow.

I decided I would go back to my home state of New Jersey and voluntarily raise my child alone before I really fucked Raheem's ass up. I wasn't going to stick around so this asshole could attempt to play me out. My car needed too many repairs, so I purchased a bus ticket to get out of there as soon as possible. I had a ticket for a Greyhound bus leaving at ten p.m., so Raheem asked if I would stop by around four p.m. so we could exchange contact information.

I pulled into his driveway where he and his best friend were having a conversation. We exchanged information, and I got back in my car to pull away. Raheem asked me to wait as he made a phone call. Afterward, a woman quickly walked out of his front door and rushed to his si   de.

"This is my new gal," Raheem said, "and she is going to have my first child." He was gesturing like he was doing some Jamaican dance; he threw his pointed fingers up in the air and began to sing, "It wasn't—"

Before he could get the "me" out, I saw shit flying from the side of his face because I had hopped out my car and punched him in the side of his mouth. I didn't stop there; I just started beating his ass up. All the anger that had been building because of the shit I had heard he was saying about my pregnancy came out with each punch.

My uncle, who was over six feet tall, rushed between us, but he didn't stop me from hopping over and around him to land another punch. Then my mother rushed over and started preaching about God and about guys putting "Spanish fly" in girls' drinks and saying, "I told you so." To address her, I ended the drama by throwing my cell phone into Raheem's forehead.

During my mother's rant, she felt the need to say, "You need to listen to me. I'm the one who took care of you when no one else wanted to."

"NO," I said. "I took care of you. That was my housing, my food stamps, and my government check, BITCH."

Later that night, I got on that Greyhound bus headed back to my home state of New Jersey.

Baby Mama Memoirs

May 14, 2001, 10:31 a.m.

Aunt Addison came home around ten a.m. She asked me if I knew a 501 area code number that was on the caller Id. I listened to the message. It was Raheem wishing me a happy Mother's Day. His message was a shock to me, Mother's Day. I was about to be a mother, and I didn't have shit—I didn't have a place that my child and I could call home; I didn't have a car to take my child to the doctor; and I didn't have a father for my child. I didn't understand what was wrong with me. If anybody ever told me no or "You can't," I made it my business to do the best for myself. But it seems that I have forgotten how to grasp control of defining myself. I didn't want to be in New Jersey.

I wanted to go to a state where nobody knew me so I would be able to reason out why I was alone. I called and spoke to Raheem about his message, but the conversation didn't change anything.

I knew what I had to do: I had to stop feeling sorry for myself and stop expecting people, I think should care the most, to give a damn about my issue.

May 15, 2001, 12:23 a.m.

The morning after my first Mother's (to Be) Day, I am so damn tired from helping Aunt Brenda with her son's birthday party, because I did everything from babysitting, to fixing plates, to cutting cake, to cleaning up.

Staying that busy was a good way to keep my

mind off of Raheem. Every day, I try to avoid thinking about my Raheem issues and crying. God, I want to stop crying; I want to know why I had to have the baby alone. What have I done so wrong to Raheem that would make him not give a fuck that I was carrying his child? God, I just want to stop crying.

I promise God that, if you'd bless me with a healthy child, I wouldn't bother Raheem, and I wouldn't ask for support or anything that would bring confusion.

God, I just want to know why my child and I have to be alone, why we aren't fit to be part of a loving family. I have a headache and my vision is blurred from all the tears. Again I am asking, "What did I do? Why can't I have a normal family? God, please help me."

May 16, 2001, 11:18 p.m.

I don't want to write in my journal using a red pen, but I have to do something fast before the tears start rolling down. Damn, I was sitting for about four hours, trying to keep my mind from wandering. I called almost all the numbers in my cell phone—even people I didn't care to talk too. Finally, I broke down and called Raheem, but of course, he was with his new girlfriend, and I didn't feel like being the needy baby mama, so I told him I would call some other time.

No matter if I'm in Arkansas, New Jersey, or Texas, my reality is that I'm alone. So I prefer to be in Texas where I will be alone because I chose to be that way. I can't believe my baby daddy didn't want to hold my growing belly, rub my sore back and neck, and hold my hand while window-shopping for the baby. Instead, I have an asshole that doesn't give a fuck if I lose my baby. Why me? I never cheated on any of my boyfriends or messed with any married men, but I still got someone who didn't measure up to a man during hard times.

Lord, I want my child with all my heart and soul, but I wonder why I wasn't blessed with a man that has the same, loving feelings about my child and me so I would have some type of family.

May 17, 2001, 12:51 p.m.
I called and spoke to my older friend Betty Jo at work. She told me that Raheem was talking shit, asking, "How many times can you tell someone you don't want them (referring to me)?"

After speaking to Betty Jo, I called Raheem and told him that I wasn't fucked up over him—someone who didn't have the heart to man up for my child and I. I want to call him again, but fuck him.

May 23, 2001, 5:00 p.m.
I went for my three-month checkup. That damn clinic made me sit there for two hours and five minutes waiting to be seen for a checkup. I hate the clinic, because I can't get any personal attention or even enough face time to ask questions. It's all I can afford, being an unemployed, single mom as a result of Raheem's lying ass.

You see, Raheem promised to pay half for the monthly checkups that cost approximately two hundred dollars. Understand, I was only asking for half or one hundred dollars per month. We agreed he would send me a money order or check stating that the money is for the baby checkup. After Raheem discussed it with friends and family, as usual, he made a 180-degree turn. Once again, I believed Raheem's lying ass and left myself open to getting my feelings hurt, but hopefully that will be the last time.

Well, anyway, the nurse took my blood pressure, and the doctor used a machine to try to find my baby's heartbeat. Before he started, he explained that they might not be able to find the heartbeat yet and not to worry. But for a brief three seconds or so, we heard the baby's heartbeat, which was one of the happiest moments I had since I was blessed with this child. I was so happy that the long wait didn't matter and I forgot about all the bullshit Raheem was putting me through.

I went to call him, which meant using my cell phone even though it had no more free daytime minutes in my plan for the month. Then I took a second to think and accept reality: I couldn't make Raheem love our baby, and if I called him, I would just be setting myself up for more pain and hurt from him. Every time, I thought about how our baby had become my baby, it made me cry. I am done writing for the day because the tears have started, and I know the headache will follow.

I wanted to be civil. I even wrote Raheem a letter that was never sent.

Letter to Raheem

Hey Raheem,

What's up? Here's the picture I promised to send. The ultrasound confirmed that I am twelve weeks and three days along with an expected due date of December 5, 2001. The checkup in Arkansas gave me an expected due date of December 2, 2001. The doctor said that the baby's heartbeat was fine.

If you notice in the picture the baby is upside down. I told the doctor that it was because the baby's father has a big head and that runs on his side of the family—just a joke, but behind every joke lies a bit of the truth.

Tell your grandmother I said "Hi" and to keep the baby and me in her prayers and next to her red clothe. After only hearing your one-sided stories, she is probably acting like the rest of your family and friends.

Let me stop because I think your sweet grandma is the only one who is willing to try to understand my concerns.

Well, by the next ultrasound (at five or six months), they can tell the sex of the child; however, I don't want to know.

Six months and counting: It seems like time is going slow; maybe it's because I'm counting by the day. Well, that's all the current baby news. Keep yourself together 'cause if it's God's will, after a DNA test, you'll be a daddy no matter what everyone around you says.

Peace,

KIA

Baby Mama Memoirs

May 27, 2001, 12:25 p.m.

I only had six dollars to my name this morning. I was hungry and having hunger pains, so I walked to Bob's Meat Market and bought a sixty-cent piece of meat to eat with some grits. When I got back, I couldn't even fix the food, because I started thinking about how we hadn't used a condom, so we had basically planned the child and we had wanted one. I had said I wanted to wait another year or so before having a child. Now my car, job, and bank account are all gone because I am three months and five days pregnant, and I have no support from Raheem.

Raheem is living the good life. He has his new girlfriend, whom he sends shopping in the mall, and here I am at the store just pricing maternity pants because none of my pants will button up. That leaves me with one pair of pink sweatpants and two pairs of workout pants. That bitch gets door-to-door pickup service from Raheem, and I am collecting every nickel and dime for bus fare to get to and from the doctor's office.

I have doctors' bills from Arkansas to New Jersey, and Raheem and his bitch are going on weekend trips to Memphis and Mississippi to gamble. He is buying all kinds of DVDs for that bitch's apartment.

Those fuckers get to sleep in until noon three to five times a week, and I am waking up at seven a.m. hungry and only able to afford a sixty-cent piece of meat.

I am going to Texas with nothing, because just like in Arkansas, I don't have shit in New Jersey. If I make it, I make it; if I don't ... well, then, fuck it. They say that what doesn't kill you will make you stronger, and right now, I am walking a very thin line. It is hard, but I know what the reality_is: I need to be prepared to be the only one willingly involved with my baby's birth, the first Christmas, the first Easter, the first step, the first word, the first birthday, and so on.

My goal was for my baby to have a family, and Raheem's goal is for his new bitch to have his first child; that will be his family. I am not waiting for him to reconsider, because time waits for no man and neither will my child and I.

By the way, I boiled that sixty-cent piece of meat, took two slices of wheat bread, added some cheese, relish, and mustard, and finally cut that meat in half and had myself two sandwiches that were damn good. If all I have to spend is sixty cents a day, I just might make it after all.

May 30, 2001

It was the final straw. Raheem called last night like he promised. He left a message talking about how he wants to be there for the baby and step up to help me more. At first I was happy that he had finally kept one of his promises, but then I started thinking about how my baby was going to wonder why his daddy only saw him a few times a year. If his new bitch had a baby as planned, her child would have a full-time daddy.

My child was worth 100 percent. It was not fair that only I had to give up my car and clear my bank accounts to try to prepare for a baby when hadn't made this baby alone.

I called Raheem's house, and his punk-ass cousin wouldn't give him the phone. No woman carrying a baby should have to go through this kind of bullshit with the father of the child and his family when she's the only one trying to care for the baby.

When I called Raheem again, his new girlfriend answered the phone, so when Raheem got on the phone, he rudely said, "What do you want, 'cause I'm sleepy." Who the fuck did he think he was talking to like that-- trying to show off in front of this bitch? I started crying and yelling while telling him off. "I don't have to put up with this shit," he said and hung up and took his house phone off the hook.

All the time I was with him, I had never seen him hang up on Shekeeda, a girl who had two kids he had raised for five years until DNA proved that they were not his. I sat and cried for about four hours. I cried, because I knew I was carrying a child for a sorry asshole who didn't give a fuck about my feelings, and I knew I had to make myself leave him alone.

It was about eight p.m. when I realized I had just sat in the house all evening and cried. I finally called Shay and asked her how she had dealt with a man who had started dating and providing for another woman while at the same time saying, "Fuck you and your baby." Whatever she said didn't stop the pain, but it was just good to know that someone understood what I was going through. Shay wasn't able to talk me off the edge but she sat on the edge with me till I was able to calm down and get back to reality.

May 31, 2001

God, if you don't help me, we'll die. I don't have anyone but you.

My mom stop believing in me a long time ago, and I don't think I really ever had a family, just the illusion. The last person I thought you would send would be Omar, but God, you have to send someone, 'cause I'm at my breaking point. Lord, I can hardly hold my head up. Raheem doesn't want anything to do with our baby or me. I don't have any money, a car, a job, or even a roof for my baby."

I came back to Lakewood because I was scared. I wanted to know how the women before me survived it; instead, all I got was the truth. The truth is that everyone turned his or her back on my child and me, especially Aunt Addison. I saw Aunt Addison like a second mother when I left my mother's house, but the reality for Addison was that I wouldn't be of any benefit to her anymore. You see I lived with her at a time when Aunt Addison wanted some additional type of adult role model in the house.

Three years later, things were looking up for Cory and Addison, and the kids were of age, so there was no need for me anymore (I'll call that the "Dick Before Chicks" protocol), just like my mother did when I no longer had a check coming into the house. You see, as long as I was in special education classes and my mother was receiving that five hundred and something-dollars government check every month, I was around to provide the basics, like a roof. But when you stop benefitting a person, they'll throw you to the dogs in the street and spit on your name.

Lord that was the second time it had happened, so

that meant I must not have passed the test the first time. I had run from one illusion to another, and I didn't want to repeat that a third time, especially not with my child. I knew I had to accept the fact that I didn't have anyone but God who would save me.

I took the first step; I erased every name in my cell phone even the names of people I wanted in my life, right down to my mom, Raheem, Aunt Addison, etc. I understood that those people didn't want me in their lives unless I could prove to them that I had something to offer. I was not mad at them; I just truly didn't have anything of value for them.

It hurts to know the truth, and the painful part is comparing my illusion to my reality. My illusion was that these people were God sent angels.

They were angels in the physical sense in that they were blessings in my life, protectors to hold my hand. Reality was simply that I had lied to myself because I didn't want to accept the fact that I had benefitted them at certain times in their lives and that had been the only reason for my presence. Now that moment has passed.

June 16, 2001

So much happened within the few weeks after I left New Jersey for Texas, but I didn't have the motivation to write about it.

I never thought of myself as a suicide case, but every day it got harder and harder to keep hope for the next day. Some days, I had to force myself to eat, and I didn't want to be around people or have them look at my face. I know everyone saw what I saw when I looked in the mirror: a pregnant girl with nothing for

her or her child and a dumb-ass who dated a man-
child who hauled ass when she got pregnant and didn't
even claim her unborn child. They saw a homeless
pregnant girl with no stable place to lay her head.

I had lived in three different states and in the
houses or apartments of more than nine different
family members and friends; I was still homeless, so it
must have been me. My mother liked to make herself
look good by putting me down and talking about me,
unless I was giving her some money. Betty Jo just
wanted me to stay with her so she could have a puppet,
keep up with the latest gossip, and make some money
on the side at the same time. Aunt Addison simply
didn't need me around anymore, because her kids were
bigger and she didn't need a babysitter or someone to
run errands anymore. I knew I was walking a thin
line with Omar, because we had never been close or cool,
and I could tell that he didn't really want me there; he
had just offered out of pity. I know he was shocked
when I took him up on it.

June 21, 2001, 7:00 p.m.
The other morning, I called Raheem, and of
course, he acted like Mr. Asshole, so I knew that his
bitch was there. He told me that his bitch had gotten
mad and left the room when I called and that I was
trying to break up his home. First, I had to explain to
him that I hadn't been fucking a married man or
someone else's man when I had gotten pregnant, so
just because his coward bitch ass didn't want to man
up and move on didn't mean I had to respect the new
shit that he was doing.

I had to get it together for my child. My child in

the womb needed me to get a grip right then, not after the sperm donor got DNA test results or after my family saw me get back on my feet. "Lord," I prayed, "please protect and bless my child while Mommy is mad as hell. Amen."

After the Rain, Texas 2001

A major storm hit Houston, Texas. The hurricane made national news with all the flooding and power outages. Luckily, my brother's second-floor apartment and the development didn't have any major flooding, but the power and communication was another issue.

Once the cell phone towers were back up and running, the first call I received was from a frantic Raheem, who was enquiring about my housing situation and the baby because of the major storm. I informed him that we were good,_and he proceeded to apologize for not being more supportive and promised that, if I returned to Arkansas for him to be there for the birth of his child, things would be better for both of us. A day or so later, Omar gave me a bullshit story about being evicted if he didn't get an extra five hundred dollars, and I knew that was my "get-the-fuck-out" hint. With my limited funds, I had to borrow an extra ten dollars from my friend Mona to purchase my bus ticket back to Arkansas.

July 8, 2001, 10:28 p.m.

So far every time I have written in this journal I was crying and all messed up in the head. Well, I'm still broke and I could still go for a little more to eat, but I'm not crying and I don't have a headache.

I went back to Arkansas on Saturday June 30, 2001, and within three days of getting there, I found myself without a bed again. I went crying to Uncle Leroy, and he offered me a place on his couch until I could get on my feet. I must say that even though I mostly slept sitting up on the love seat, I was getting some good sleep.

Before I came back to Arkansas, I asked God to give me the strength to face and deal with my demons. When I say demons, I'm referring to my feelings of embarrassment and failure when I had to face all the people I trusted and thought would have had my back—number one being the fucker I made a child with and then my mother, aunts, and cousins. Keeping it real, I had come back because I wanted my child to have a father. I was very confused because I didn't know what a good father was or looked like, and I prayed that I hadn't fuck up and made a baby with a man-child.

All the bullshit that had gone down during my few months of pregnancy was proof that I was on the road to some crazy baby mama bullshit, so I was trying to refocus my attention. But every day, I woke up knowing that I had nothing, and that left me with only the option of fucking Raheem's ass up. The taunts and laughter from my family members were adding to my fury. Every day, I got a quick glance of Raheem, and I made myself put my head down or look the other way, because I didn't want to give him the pleasure of seeing the pain in my face. Every time I saw him, I thought about the fact that Raheem fooled me into coming back and wouldn't put the time into helping me while I was carrying our child. However, he had plenty of time to put into his new ugly-ass girlfriend.

The thought of him with someone else, happy... and me alone because I chose to have my child, used to make me cry for three to five hours at a time. Then I heard this church song that said, "Take it to Jesus, only he can give you peace." I wanted to give this hurt to anyone but me. Later on that day, I saw an interview with some rapper, and he stated that when things get bad and everyone leaves and you have to do it by yourself, it must be a great task. Then I started to realize that I'm not the only one; I'm just one of the chosen few who can handle the task. That sounded good, so I kept telling myself that to help me accept being kicked to the curb after getting pregnant.

July 10, 2001

On July 9, Raheem came over, and we talked mostly about bullshit. He told me that he and his girlfriend were having issues about my calling him. He wanted to have a sit-down conversation with all of us, but I had to promise not to fight anyone. I told him I didn't make promises I couldn't keep.

August 13, 2001

I hated writing in my journal, because it just proved that I didn't have anybody on my side or anyone who cared to listen to me. So much bullshit happened that it made me depressed to even think about it. August 12 was Raheem's grandma's birthday. I wasn't shocked, and it is still hurtful that his aunts and family members showed their true colors. Half of those bitches looked me dead in my face and didn't speak. I knew what the deal was. First, they were in public (you see, they only talk to me behind closed doors and over the phone). Second, the new girlfriend was present and they had to prove their loyalty to Raheem.

They all got a good laugh but that wouldn't happen again, because I won't fuck with any of them again. As for Raheem ... fuck him and fuck him again. That bastard not only tried to hit me, he did knee me in my stomach the last time we got into it, trying to prove bitch-hood to his girl. Once again, I showed him how a real bitch beats ass. Yeah, I prayed and cried at night and then punched him in the morning, but my dumb ass baby daddy couldn't get it that he was trying to go toe-to-toe with someone who had lost everything. All I could do was release my pain in my punches. As long as his bitch kept her mouth closed I would stick to only fucking up the asshole I was pregnant by.

Raheem had the nerve to tell me that he was not going to pay the six hundred dollars for a DNA test that will prove the baby is his, because that's too much. But money was no object when it came to doing things for his ugly bitch: buying that bitch a car, moving her in, and going on weekend trips. That bitch didn't go to work much anymore, and my baby daddy didn't have an issue with spending his money to take care of her grown ass.

My body was sore, and I was so tired, but I didn't even have a bed to sleep in. I was only working as a substitute teacher and an on-call janitor cleaning the board of education offices, still trying to stack up on diapers, wipes, and other baby supplies. The sooner I accepted the fact that I couldn't give my baby a family, the sooner I could stop fooling myself. For six and a half months I had been lying to myself and trying to make excuses for Raheem's absence, but there was no excuse for Raheem to not fucking care about the child I was carrying.

September 11, 2001

I was told to keep a diary to deal with stress and depression from not having my baby's father to support me during my pregnancy. All the time, I thought about Raheem and about being alone (which was every day) during my pregnancy. I was supposed to write my feelings in my diary. However, writing in the diary was more depressing, because it meant admitting that I was alone. Even though I had others in my presence, the only person I wanted to be with during my pregnancy was Raheem, because that's how it's supposed to be, but Raheem didn't want me. September 11 was one of the few times I had written in my diary without crying or being depressed. I think I finally got it.

Even though it took me seven months of a pregnancy full of crying, worrying, fighting, and God knows what else, I finally understood that I couldn't make Raheem feel honored that I was having his child; I finally understood that my child didn't have a daddy.

My whole objective for moving down south had been to give my child something I had always wanted and had never gotten: a father's touch.

I had some really screwed up feelings when it came to dealing with Raheem. You know, they say there's a thin line between love and hate, and my friend Dirty was always saying that I was in love with Raheem, but Dirty was wrong. I wanted to have love for the man I was having a child with, but how can a woman and mother fix her damn mouth to say she loves a baby daddy who doesn't care about her or the child she's carrying?

Raheem pitied himself, and the only way to love him would be out of pity not respect. You see, Raheem was very smart; he knew that, if a woman loved him out of pity, she would have to accept all his excuses for the things he did to her (e.g., lying and cheating) because of the pity she had for him. I guess the pity game did get Raheem some pussy; it got him mine for a minute. The self-pity game he played came with a cost, and that cost was his manhood, which he had to keep trying to prove to everyone around, because he had not defined or proven it to himself.

Consequently, our child was the perfect example. In my heart and mind, I already knew that we both had different reasons for wanting the child. I had wanted a child with Raheem because I thought he was smart, hardworking, and sensitive. I thought those characteristics would make him into a husband and father in the near future. His reason for messing around and fucking with me was to show off to the boys in the hood and be the first to say he had gotten some East coast ass. Raheem hadn't picked me to be his wife or the mother of his child because I was smart, hardworking, and cute—I was just another piece of ass he was having raw sex with, like he had been doing for the past seven years, praying that one day his weak ass soldiers would work.

Once the baby was made and coming, he was not

concerned about us being a family or about him being the father that would always be there. His main concern was once again to prove to everyone around him (his own broke-ass father, his male cousins, and mostly his ex-girlfriend) that he was a real man who was capable of producing a child—the hell with the providing part of being a parent. Hell, I did all the work while he just lay there anyway. While he was so busy proving his manhood to his fellow peers, he was not focusing on being there and helping me to bring the baby into the world.

I was not going to cheat my child because Radio Raheem was too busy with his friends, his phony family, and his ugly new girlfriend. I would find a man who wanted us to support each other while we both focused on the child, one who would be there all night to assist with feedings & checkups and discuss what, when, and how to handle family matters. Maybe I was asking for too much, because if the man whose blood was running through the child didn't care, could I expect God to send another man to care and give us a 100 percent? I would not accept a drop-in daddy who just wanted to show friends and family that the baby had his hair, eyes, or feet: My child and I needed and deserved the best.

September 13, 2001

I finally got a break. I would prefer to be at home like the doctor said, but I had my baby to think about. On September 13th I felt dizzy and light-headed. My stomach was hurting, and working with some smart-mouthed children wasn't helping. I thanked God I was able to keep a few dollars in my pocket, because unlike my first and second trimester, hunger pains couldn't be put off for a few days. I spoke with Raheem the day before. He told me that he wanted four kids by four different women, not including the child I was carrying, because he wanted to sign over his parental rights and have nothing to do with my child.

Like most punks, he said my kid was not his because he was sterile; but I was pregnant with a child he claimed was not his. Still based on my pregnancy, he thought his soldiers would work somewhere else. Anyway, I told him to get the paperwork; I would gladly agree to him signing off his paternal rights.

September 20, 2001, 10:27 p.m.

I had my first Braxton Hicks contraction, so I expected to not get a lot of sleep. Sleeping on the couch had become very uncomfortable due to my growing baby and belly. I asked my boy, Dirty to be my birthing coach if I got settled enough to get to that point. All this time, I had been rejecting his support because I wanted Raheem to be with me, but I had to stop fooling and lying to myself. I was too tired to write anything about that lying bastard and how he was treating me while I was carrying his child.

Homeless & Keeping You Head Up

It seems like everybody you meet and on TV has a homeless story from their past, but no one tells the details of how they got to that point. So are you considered homeless because you don't have your own home or because you're sleeping on someone's couch or because you're sleeping outside? Why?

After I returned to Arkansas, my baby daddy pulled a fucking whammy. He called himself making it clear that the only way he was going to be supportive during my pregnancy was if I agreed to live with him and his new girlfriend.

"It don't matter as long as I'm the girlfriend," the bitch said.

"Hell fucking no," I said, "I don't share shit, especially dick, bitch. I'll sleep in the street before I let your bitch ass play me like some trick at a truck stop" Be careful of what you say; you better mean it.

When I turned to my family—(which was my mother with a three-bedroom mobile home, my sister with a two-bedroom apartment, and my aunt with a three-bedroom mobile home), they gladly let me know that now I had a degree but no baby daddy. What a degree and a baby daddy have to do with each other... I didn't know they were passing out daddies with degrees. With their smirks and taunts, they made it very clear that I was not a welcome member of the family circle and that I wasn't welcomed in their trailers, houses, or apartments.

On my way to the women's shelter, I stopped by my Uncle Leroy's house to ask if I could store some of my items in his shed. He asked me where was I going, and I told him I was going to the women's shelter. He invited me to stay on his couch, and I gladly accepted.

During the first few weeks on the couch at my new home, I got temporary jobs working as an elementary school substitute teacher during the day and as an on-call janitor at the school district administration building in the evening.

In the meantime, my baby daddy, who lived two

houses away, was happily taking care of his new girlfriend who worked at Wal-Mart, and I was starting to receive telephone threats from his female friends, who said that they were going to beat my child out of my stomach. To make matters worse, my crack-head cousin decided to start coming over at two and three in the morning to watch porn and jerk off in front of me in the room I was sleeping in. I heard a saying in the South that "cousins make a dozen," but in my world, a "cousin can get cut the fuck up."

So the first chance I could, with a handled knife tucked at my side, I moved from my nightly home on the couch into the front seat of my '85 red Chevy Nova (which didn't have insurance because my helpful sister charged me to add me to her insurance but just kept my money and went to a damn Janet Jackson concert). Next, every time I sat and dwelled on the raw reality of my situation, I would walk over to my baby daddy's house and whip his ass.

I also went to make these ass-kicking visits after receiving calls from his female bitches, which were talking shit or threatening to bring harm to my unborn child.

I sent out a lot of personal invitations to many bitches for the opportunity to get fucked up by a pregnant chick. Finally, I worked at my two temp jobs, read parenting books, studied for the GRE test, and kept a big smile on my face during the day.

During the night, I cried, prayed, and cried some more until I fell asleep at various hours of the morning. Don't think of me as a pity case just because I lived in a car up until my eighth month of pregnancy; with my knife at my side, I would adjust my Wal-Mart body pillow (which cost $8.88) against the driver's side door and under my belly and got some good sleep for the few hours that I did sleep. Hell, I kept myself together and took my showers in my uncle's house at a decent hour before his son came over.

I changed my weave every two weeks at Dirty's or my aunt's house; my clothes were always coordinated, neat, and clean. My dirty clothes were bagged to the right side of the trunk, undergarments were in the middle of the trunk, and clean clothes were folded on the left side of my car's trunk.

Normal Dysfunctional Family

Being that my mother and father were never married it was very easy for me to distinguish the difference of my "Mother's Side" of the family and my "Father's Side" of the family. I was tightly raised with my mother's side of the family and no matter how much I tried to hang with my older cousins, I really never fit in with my family's routine of doing things. My mother's side of the family consists of some tough-talking, ass-kicking, do or die type of chicks and even though I had participated in my share of fist fights, being a "school-girl" had characterized me as the "punk" of the family.

I didn't view school involvement as something for the smartest person, but as a game of survival for the most strategic person; instead of releasing my pain on the streets like some of my family members, I released mines within the walls of schools.

Pursing a college degree further polarized me within my family and it became clearly evident when one of my female cousins, became the first person to ever pull a gun on me. I also was physically jumped twice by some of my other female cousins during my college years. The crazy thing about my family is that if someone else on the street tried to fight me, they would run to my aid, so this dysfunctional trend was normal in my family life. Although I wasn't in Jersey with my many cousins, I would soon learn that my family's dysfunction still ran deep even in the south.

Hair Do's and Don'ts

What could be worse than being pregnant, sleeping in your car, having your baby daddy and his new girlfriend pull up every morning after picking her up from her graveyard shift at Wal-Mart, then having them spend a few moments pointing and laughing at you and enduring the humiliation of your immediate family members taunting and ridiculing you worse than your biggest enemy would? I couldn't understand how several family members in New Jersey, Texas, and Arkansas could turn their backs on me with the attitude that "You get what you deserve, bitch." The hurtful thing was that I knew it had to be me, but I didn't know what exactly had brought it out in my family members. I just assumed it was my big mouth and my too-cute attitude, but the whole family had these characteristics, so why was I being singled out and ostracized for it. There's a saying that states "the truth shall set you free," but it can get you fucked up too.

I already mentioned how I spent my days as though my current situation was just a mere technicality. What I didn't know was that the haters in my family couldn't handle how I still acted like I was "The Shit". This was after being publicly humiliated by my baby daddy, while sleeping in a car and working as an on-call janitor with a damn business degree. What else could I do? I wasn't ready to die, so I had to make the most of what I had to work with.

When it was time for me to renew my two-week hairdo, Dirty had some female company for the evening, so I was going to ask my aunt if I could go into her trailer and wash my hair when I finished taking my braids out. When I walked up her wooden steps, my cousin met me at the door and told me that her mom was gone and that she was about to do her hair. That was no big deal. I still needed to take my hair out anyway, so I figured I would just wait until Dirty was chilling alone at home and use his place.

It was still early in the evening, and I sat on my uncle's couch watching a TV show. My intoxicated aunt Betty busts through the door and rushed into my uncle's room as if she was looking for him. Then she rushed to me and stood over me.

"I Will Kill You, Bitch," she slurred at me.

I couldn't move. She was already standing over me with her hand cuffed under her left breast, so the first thing I did was grab my big belly to protect my unborn child and tuck my head into my chest.

The next words that came out of her mouth were "If you move, you will be having that baby tonight." I sat there frozen in shock and scared as hell. The tears started running from my eyes; because I had no doubt that she had come in ready to fuck me up; But why? As my fifty-year-old inebriated aunt stood over me, ranting about me going into her house to do my napping hair, she called me all kinds of things—stupid, black, ugly, dumb special-education, punk bitches—and then I guess her buzz or adrenaline high wore off. She took a seat on the couch across from me, but she never took her hand from under her left breast.

Understand that my family has a long reputation for cutting people, and it was rumored that this aunt proudly cut another lady's breast off in her younger days.

I stayed in my crouched position, holding my belly and looking at the floor as the steady flow of tears soaked the collar of my shirt.

"You thought you was something," she started. "Going to college, thinking you were better than folks, Look at you now. You ain't got shit and still act like you're better than folks—reading books—and everyone knows you sleep in a damn car." She went on for another fifteen minutes or so until she finally said, "The next time you need to do your hair, just ask first." All I could think was, "What the fuck?" For the last thirty minutes, I have been in a frozen position, scared for my life. I eased my eyes up to look at her and slowly removed my hands from my belly. I pulled my hair scarf off to unveil my braided hair.

"Okay," I said softly.

She stood up and walked out through the back door of the house, calmly and coolly. To put the icing on the cake for the night, guess what happened next? My uncle walked out of his room, which was only three feet away. "Damn, that bitch is crazy as hell," he said. "She needs to stop drinking so damn much."

I asked him where he had come from, and he told me he had been in his room the whole time and had just been listening to see what she was going to do. My uncle would have let me get fucked up just so he could be the first to gossip about what happened. That really showed me that I didn't have anybody in my corner, but I still didn't want to believe it.

"What doesn't kill you will make you stronger"; people say that all the time, and usually we don't want to hear it or even understand it. When reflecting on my past pregnancy, I can't help but think about some of the things that I thought were the end of the world—they are just memories now. After my father's funeral my aunt Betty pulled me to the side and said, " If I ever did anything wrong to you I want to apologize."

The sad thing about it was that I don't think she even remember the fearful details of 'the night I thought would be my last over a damn degree,' at that moment she gave me her "sincere" apology.

Baby Mama Memoirs

September 26, 2001, 11:27 p.m.

September 26 was the first day that it was all about my unborn child. Things in my life were still fucked up, and in some ways, they were more fucked up than before, but no matter how bad things were going, I was happy for a whole day. I had another doctor's appointment in the last two weeks of my pregnancy. The baby had grown a lot. My son was sixteen inches long by then, and his head was down. He was getting ready for the real world.

October 16, 2001, 10:08 p.m.

I called Raheem, for what I don't know; probably just to hear him talk the same shit on a different day. He came over on Friday and talked for about two and a half hours. He had come over to tell me to find someone else and that I should let him go so he and his new bitch could get on with their lives. Then he called his mother and sister over to join the meeting. After all that talk about how I needed to let him go, that punk felt my ass as I walked into my uncle's house. The only reason he did that was to keep me looking like some love-crazed fool (for an ego booster). If I hadn't been so tired, I would have turned around and shown him how I had let go by letting my fist go straight into his jaw, (for all the shit that he hadn't done for me). Shit like that was why I hated him.

Dirty said the only reason I hated him was because I was in love with him and he didn't love me. Whatever!

I didn't think it was Raheem I loved; however, I always dreamed that my child would be made in love. I always dated and fucked men who seemed to be the type of men who were fit to be full-time dads and who respected the women who would bear their children.

Thank God for Government Housing

When I had returned to Arkansas in June, I had applied for any and all types of housing programs. In mid-September, I got a call that my lottery number had been chosen and that I needed to go in to get pre-qualified for an apartment. The housing complex was in a new development that used to be a drug and gang-infested project. The projects had been demolished, so the screening process would now be very vigorous. I had all of my paperwork ready. However, my current job status was an issue, so I read all the fine print of the application and found out that attending school within the past twelve months was enough to qualify me for an apartment. For the first time since I had graduated, my bachelor's degree had a benefit … getting me some government housing.

On November 1st, I moved from my car into a brand-new, two-bedroom, duplex apartment with a washer, dryer, and a driveway Unlike most people I knew who went to the local Rental to Buy store to rent some overpriced bullshit, I went and purchased a living room set from the Aaron's repossession section in the back of the store for $250 in cash and then made my way to local secondhand thrift stores and indoor flea markets to buy lamps, dressers, and a queen size bed. I was going into my ninth month of pregnancy when I moved into the apartment, and

I refused to tell anyone about my new living situation until the baby was born. They were having such a good time laughing at me living out of my car that I didn't want to disturb their entertainment.

A House Is Not a Home

You would have thought that a brand-new, rent-controlled apartment would have brought me some peace of mind, but I was still sad and depressed. I still pondered over being a single mother and about Raheem's ill feelings towards my unborn child, because it was my child. I looked forward to taking the DNA test he now didn't even want to take. Raheem asked if he could come to see the birth. I agreed, even though, if I could have moved my legs after my C-section, I would've kicked his ass in that hospital room.

You would have thought that being a single mother would leave me no time to bother Raheem, but I still made it my business to show my ass. I remember one day, I asked if he had a few dollars so I could pick up some baby water.

"I gave you a five-hundred-dollar crib, so I'm not giving you my money," he said. "And I want the crib back when my girl has the baby I really wanted." I went home and tore that solid wooden crib to pieces, put it in a bag, drove to his house, and threw the crib pieces and a shitty diaper all over his porch. When he and his girl came to the door, I happily yelled, "Here's your shit back," got back into my car, and drove away feeling content for the moment.

After the birth of the baby, Raheem's ugly girlfriend felt it was time to show her ass. She called me and said, "I wish you would've had a miscarriage, but it's not too late for SIDS."

"You know," I said, "I'm going to fuck you up, and I don't care how long it takes for me to get to you. All I ask is that you take the ass-whipping I'm going to give you like the woman you think you are, okay?" Then I simply hung up.

My grandma passed away in February, and I gladly jumped at an opportunity to go to New Jersey. Ironically, this occurred right before we were ready to leave the state: The results of the DNA test arrived in the mail confirming that Raheem was the father.

When we arrived in New Jersey, the baby and I stayed at my Aunt Addison's house for about three months, and I could tell that my aunt wasn't keen on us being there. I knew that because my aunt's house had always had an open-door policy— everyone in our family from brothers, nieces, cousins, and their kids to their boyfriends, had stayed with our aunt. When she wanted someone gone, she would stop speaking and start slamming things around the house with a get-the-fuck-out attitude. Even though I had lived with my aunt for four years before, I had never felt the full wrath of her attitude, because I had always been a benefit to the house ... but that was before I had a baby on my hip. In an effort to save face, I proudly let it be known that I had a brand-new apartment, so I didn't need to be sleeping on someone's floor. With that, I made my way to Trenton and caught a train back down south to return to my lonely miserable life. I didn't want to go back. I was scared, and in New Jersey, I had family and friends, and I knew the lay of the land. But knowing that we weren't welcomed in Aunt Addison's home left me with no other option but to return to Arkansas.

The stakes got higher when I returned to Arkansas. I informed Raheem when I would return, and he asked if I would bring the baby, since he hadn't seen him for a few months. So around nine thirty a.m., I had a neighbor pick me up from the train station and take me down to my uncle's house so I could get my car. While I was letting my car warm up, I walked over to Raheem's door and rang the doorbell. When there was no answer, I proceeded back to my car. The next thing I heard was a gunshot and my neighbor throwing herself to the ground. I turned to see my baby daddy waving a gun. I calmly strapped my child into his car seat and walked back up to the porch. This incident is currently in court, so in an effort not to incriminate myself, all I can write down is that the confrontation ended with my baby daddy yelling, "Don't you see I have a gun, bitch?" and me saying, "You missed, bitch."

Having a gun pulled on me with my child was a bit too much for me, so I decided that it was over. I was tired of fighting for nothing. I started desperately looking for something that could make my situation better and help me out of my bitter phase. I began saying a short simple prayer: "God, make me better and not bitter."

I tried to live an autonomous lifestyle as a new mother. My search for a job in my career field was going nowhere, and it was clear that I would need more than the bragging rights of having earned a four-year degree if I was going to provide shelter, food, and childcare for my child. Times were getting harder. To save money on my light bill in the hot southern summer, I would push my stroller throughout the mall for hours. Since I wanted to go back to school, I would also put my baby in the stroller and just walk around the local university campus, visiting office staff about twice a week.

Returning to school seemed like the most logical option, so I checked out a GRE practice book at the local library, although I remained skeptical. I knew I was a poor test-taker, and I had limited funds; even registering for the required test was a major issue. My persistence and regular college visits helped me secure an ally within the graduate school department, and her status as an intake secretary for the Graduate School department provided me with a wealth of alternative and provisional options for getting into graduate school.

June 21, 2002

There were a lot of choices that needed to be made fast. The stress of wanting to be a good mother yet having no resources was overwhelming. I decided to write my son DJ a letter about my future plans...

Hey DJ,

This week, I had to go down to the Department of Human Services to sign up for welfare and food stamps and search our home for items to take back to the store so I could try to pay our lights, gas, and phone bill. As crazy as it sounds, I can't even begin to think about this month's rent. DJ, it's been humiliating to be down in the DHS office for the past three days straight; asking them to please process my food stamp paperwork because I knew I only had three jars of baby food left.

That's why I spent my last five dollars and bought a large jar of all-natural Lucky Leaf applesauce—I won't receive any food stamps until July 5th. I didn't know what to do, so I put my pride aside, and I called Raheem three times, but he never answered.

I'm kind of glad he didn't. I shouldn't have to beg him to help me with you.

Raheem willingly took care of two kids that weren't his, but he won't help me with his real child...

you. Well, I'm not going to keep letting that make me depressed: That's why I'm writing this shit down.

I can't find a job because my degree makes me overqualified for the jobs that are hiring on the spot. I'm raising you alone with no help from Raheem's or my family down here in the South. I can't afford day care, so I can't make any money. Now that push has come to shove, I'm going to create money since I can't make any. I'm going to find a way to be a real mother who can raise and provide for her child and not one who has the child providing for the family. I'm so sorry that we have to struggle because of my stupidity, but I'm going to make up for all the mad mother mistakes that I'm making.

Love Always,

Mommy

Hollywood Hood Stars

There is no nice way to say this shit, so I'm just going to make a whole lot of fuckers mad. I always hear bitches talk about how they are handling their business and that's why some man is trying to holler, court, or just get at them. Come on, you're living in a known housing development or claiming fame to some fancy Section 8-provided housing situation while being a single mother of four or five kids and only making seven dollars an hour. You're not fooling anybody who matters. You're just the perfect target for a **man-child**, a lazy liar, or someone's cheating husband.

Once I got settled into my brand-new, low-income housing apartment, I had all kinds of males—from the professional police officer paroling the area to the local drug-dealing/car salesman's thug—trying to feed me that bullshit line about how they would love a woman like me who was "handling her business."

Handling my business—what they meant to say was that they would love a woman who wouldn't require much.

Their hope was that the rental assistance would provide housing, and the food stamps would provide them home-cooked meals for a few weeks out of the month. Thanks to state Medicaid, medical costs wouldn't be a topic of discussion. So it's not that I was the "hot chick" but more of a "cheap chick" to date. Like a married man and his mistress, all the men would have to do is come around with a few dollars for a hairdo, nails, or a designer purse and maybe put a couple of dollars on the light bill and be seen as God's gift to an "independent woman on assistance". No Thank-You.

By now, you can tell that I love to talk shit but I still had needs that a man had to handle. As a **Hollywood Hood Star**, my script went like this, "I'm not paying for no dick, and since Uncle Sam is my main man, the food stamps he gives me only feed the persons listed on the application." I didn't play. A man couldn't get a bottle of water from me. I wasn't cooking any man's damn Sunday dinner or buying meat and chips for anyone's fucking barbecue. No one was allowed to sit up in my spot and suck up my air conditioning or heat.

Suffice it to say that outside of a little dick here and there, I didn't date for the next few years. I'd rather live alone than to live a lie, so I guess I was on the D-list of Hollywood hood-stars.

Who the Hell Are You Talking To?

I was at the point that I started cutting family and friends in New Jersey and Arkansas off. My phone was mostly used for keeping time, so when it rang with an unknown Jersey number, I was a bit shocked.

"Hello?" I answered.

"What's going on down there," JoJo asked through the phone. "Why you won't let that boy see his baby?"

"WHAT?" I asked.

"Raheem has the right to see his son," JoJo said.

"WHO THE HELL ARE YOU TALKING TO?" I said, "I know my deadbeat father didn't have the nerve to call my fucking cell to tell me about my damn child. Look, bitch, try being a father first before you try pulling the grandfather card, and stay the fuck off my damn phone with this bullshit."

I slammed the phone down as I simulated hanging up in his face.

Behind Bars for Baby's Shoes

Struggling is just that, but when you can't cover the basics for that baby, there is a certain kind of hurt within your struggle. As you have already seen, I hadn't been anything close to an angel. Yes, I was guilty of a whole lot of bullshit, but on that one night, I just wanted my baby to have his first pair of Payless walking shoes, and I went to jail for that.

I was barely providing the basic necessities. I was just starting to get government assistance of foods stamp and living on housing, so designer kids' cloths and shoes weren't on the top of my priority list as a good mother. Since my child was still young, I mostly just put a pair of socks on his feet and kept it moving.

One day, I ran into the baby's grandfather (Raheem's father) at the grocery store. As he played with my child, he mentioned that he would be ready to walk soon and that I better protect his ankles so he wouldn't have any issues.

"I'll get to it when I get to it," I said.

Later that day, I received numerous calls from Raheem. When I finally answered, he quickly said that he was calling out of concern for his son. Let me remind you that I hadn't spoken to him in weeks since the gun incident. During the course of the conversation, he made a sincere plea that sounded like he wanted to help provide for the baby. He said that his father had suggested that he go ahead and purchase some walking shoes for him. At first I refused, because I didn't trust his offer, but as I thought about it, I felt that it would be selfish for me to deny something that would benefit my child just because I had bitter feelings. We made arrangements for me to pick up the shoe money that evening.

I pulled up in front of his house. With the baby still strapped in his car seat, I walked over to Raheem, who was talking on his cell phone at the door of someone's truck. I gestured for him to hurry up. As I looked around the yard at the people standing around, the whole setting felt a bit contrived.

An uneasy feeling came over me, so I said, "Fuck this... Keep that damn shoe money."

As I turned to walk back to my car, all I felt was my face hitting the gravel on the ground. Raheem had slammed me to the ground and was using his body weight to hold me down. Then he started yelling, "Call them... Call them now."

Raheem's little cousin, who had never liked me, started talking to him, saying, "Man, don't do this. What about your baby, man?" But Raheem continued to yell, "I told you, call them now. Go call them now!"

I tried moving in every direction, but his body weight was too much for me. The next thing I heard were the sirens of the approaching police cars. As the police pulled up, Raheem jumped up and ran over to them, telling them that I was trespassing and had attacked him.

Because he didn't have any marks on him, they told him that, if he wanted to press charges, they would have to arrest both of us. His simple reply was, "Go ahead and take us both in... I'll be out in a few hours, but she can't even afford shoes for her own baby, so she'll be in there for a while."

Any other day, I would have been guilty as charged, but that night, all I wanted was some shoes for my baby, and for that, I went to jail. My older cousin Mary (who was sixty years old) took my son, and it took a day and a hundred dollars borrowed from my mother for me to get out of jail. I also had to promise my entire first welfare stipend of $160 on the first of the month, to the bonds lady.

Additionally, I also had to sign over my car title to the bonds company to make my $250 bail. I had no one to call, and I was shocked to see that it was my mother working on my behalf on the outside. When I questioned her motive for helping me, she told me that Raheem had been bragging about how he had set me up. He had even come to her, happily explaining what he had done.

It was on. I had been backed into a corner, and I had no choice but to come out fighting. However, this time around, I was going to fight for *my future and me.*

I was determined to make moves to be successful as a single mother. The first of the month came, and I entered the bonds office, prepared to turn my entire first welfare stipend over. Three hours later, I had redesigned their client database and walked out with all of my money plus a little bonus. For the next six court dates, that bail bonds office helped me to tap into and development my skills as an instructor and trainer. The charges were thrown out of court before I could even walk in front of the judge. It is so crazy how you can be blessed in the midst of some mess.

The Doctor's Prescription

I really wanted to be able to take care of my child, but I couldn't find a job. So as I laid on my gynecologist's chair, trying to get my checkup while holding my baby, the gynecologist once again called one of his nurses in to take and watch the baby for me. My doctor was a short fine black man who was very kind and caring, and my checkups were also counseling sessions. During our session, I became teary-eyed as I explained my embarrassment at needing to apply for welfare benefits. Being finished with my checkup, the doctor took me back to his office to elaborate on his feelings.

"Look," he said, "the government takes money from my pay to provide welfare services, and people get stuck on those services, but it would be really nice to know that one of the clients is using those benefits to make a better life for her family. Just make a plan, and stick to it, and hold off on the second kid."

I truly admired how my doctor used his professionalism and passion to inspire me and not to insult me as so many people do once they have reached certain levels in their career status.

Being on government assistance afforded me the opportunity to attend graduate school full-time, but I planned on only using it for one year. This 1-year plan meant taking a full-time load of graduate classes, which would have been nine credits for the typical student, so I enrolled in twelve credits including a full load for the summer session.

Disappearing Act

I don't have many detailed stories from the next two years, because I went from the jailhouse to the schoolhouse and I went hard. Raheem was dead to me, so I said "fuck you" to his money too. What I had, was what I would work with.

Since I wouldn't fuck with him on any level, dear old grandma (Raheem's mother) stepped up and would sometimes get my son for a weekend or for a family Christmas dinner. Our conversations were always concise and only about DJ's visits and not about any needs. His overnight bag always had his necessities, and he was returned with them. I changed my entire routine from where I shopped for groceries to where the baby went for day care to even stop speaking to old friends and family and focus on investing in my future plans.

The family's past taunts of "You have a degree but no baby daddy" hurt me deeply, and I made sure not to let anyone in my family know about my attempting to get a master's degree.

During my first semester, I had anxiety attacks and only three to four hours of sleep daily, and that resulted in me getting seven A's and one B (one of my classes had three individual grades). By taking twelve hours per semester and throughout the summer, by the end of my first year, I had started my plan to get off government assistance by paying for my own private childcare services.

The first 10-months or so of living in my new apartment complex was spent trying to chase my baby-daddy down and crying. Now that my tears had dried up, I could see the blessing right next door at Ms. Glenda's (Granny) house. It was a shocking discovery to learn that my next-door neighbor for almost a year was also an employee at my son's state provided daycare center.

The state paid $85 a week for his daycare services and Ms. Glenda was making a mere $125 a week to care for a room of twenty or so kids. I was able to make a deal and steal Ms. Glenda from her job with an offer of $100 cash a week.

As an added incentive, I gave her an extra $20 so I could have some Saturday morning library study time, and another $20 for more Sunday afternoon library study time. There was no amount of money that could ever make up for the security of knowing that my child was treated like just another one of Granny's babies while I went to school or needed to study.

After a year and a semester I was done, but because of the graduate school's requirements of comprehensive tests and a panel review schedule, I had to stay another semester. I registered for a PhD-level statistics class and some additional graduate credits. I had traded baby-mama bullshit for books and it felt good.

"More in 2004" was my chosen motto for the New Year. Well, I did it. I rescinded the welfare benefits for my son in December 2003. I gave up my state day care voucher and paid for the private childcare that I wanted for my baby.

I worked thirty hours per week for my graduate assistant positions and for fifteen to twenty hours a week as a part-time GED instructor.

Before the first half of 2004 had past, I graduated with dual master's degrees in education, and I won every academic award that the university could offer a graduate student. Then the time came for me to take the ultimate risk and leave the safety of my government housing and move to Texas to start my career and go from being a state dependent baby mama to being an independent single mother with a career and a plan.

Right before my graduation, Raheem's lawyer had me subpoenaed to court to get custody of my son based on the fact that he and his next new girlfriend Sam were getting married. His position was that the child should be raised with two parents instead of a single mother.

I couldn't afford a lawyer, so I went to court with a letter from the Department of Human Services stating that I had rescinded the benefits that I still qualified for. When it was my turn to speak, I told the judge I that I might be a single mother but that I was moving to Texas to provide for my child.

I told him that the two-parent house that I was up against was still funded by the government's Section 8 housing program, in which my child's father illegally resided. After that day, I was issued twenty-five dollars per week in child support. Raheem laughed and volunteered an additional twenty-five dollars and was granted only visitation rights.

The Summer of Sam

I had applied to and been accepted into an alternative certification teaching program in Texas. I assumed that getting a job would be easy; I was more marketable after having completed two internships and compiling an impressive portfolio, not to mention the fact that Texas was having one of its largest turnovers of retirees. I reserved my U-Haul, secured a two-bedroom apartment, and gave my thirty-day move-out notice. The only catch was that my two-and-a-half-year-old child would have to stay behind in Arkansas because of Raheem's visitation rights. The day came when I was scheduled to leave. Raheem and his soon-to-be wife came to my vacant apartment to take away my son. It was my second time meeting Raheem's fiancée, Sam, and our encounters had always been amiable.

I left for Texas, and it only took two weeks before Sam started showing her true colors. She wouldn't let me speak to my son.

Along with Raheem, they referred to her as my child's mother, and she finally had the nerve to tell me that I should be grateful that she was raising my child. "You're his babysitter, BITCH," I said angrily, and within the next twenty-four hours, I was back in Arkansas, planning to beat that bitch's ass. Raheem and Sam drove up to my uncle's house to bring DJ to see me. I really wanted to get a good grip on the bitch, so I was inching my way toward the passenger side, where she was seated. I could tell she was scared because she rolled the window up, but little did she know that I had my Timberland boots on, and I was planning to easily burst that glass with one strong right kick. I had eased into a perfect position when my brother jumped in front of me.

"I know what you're about to do," he said, "and that's what she wants. Then it looks like you're fighting over Raheem. If you really want more in life, you have to let this bullshit go."

I didn't beat the bitch that day, and they both still tried to fuck with my head through my son. For example, they got married that August, and on the way back from their honeymoon around eleven thirty p.m., they decided to call me claiming that they wanted me to talk to my son. I replied that it was almost midnight, so my kid should be asleep in bed. Then the bitch started yelling in the background, "I'm the real Mrs. Jones. We're the Jones family." I simply replied, "Only a stupid bitch would be calling her new husband's baby mama on their honeymoon night, instead of fucking or sucking on her man. Goodnight, dumb ass." I hung up the phone.

The summer of Sam was a hard few months of me learning to keep my mouth shut and staying calm. I learned that reacting to someone's bullshit made it my bullshit. The foundation of their marriage was fucking with me, and when I refused to participate, I guess they had to play with each other. Needless to say, their marriage fell apart within a year.

A Blast from the Past

I returned to Texas and waited until my child was scheduled to be returned in August. With a few more weeks left to myself, it was nice to reconnect with a blast from the past. When he called me and told me that he was coming to Texas to see me—I was so happy. I mean he knew that he was the closest thing to the concept of "lover homie friend" for me, even though it had been about six years ago when we were in college. Now there I was, an overweight, single mother, who was bitter, alone, and trying to recover from my baby daddy doing everything to hurt me, embarrass me, and break my spirits. Now here comes Nasir, planning to fly hundreds of miles just to see me.

There I was trying to figure out what was wrong with me, why I didn't or couldn't have a man who really cared about my well being and would take the time, effort, and money to prove his interest and sincerity for me. Being realistic, I knew that Nasir's trip was not the same as being together as man and wife, but his trip was like a sign of hope for me that a man was willing to make time for me in his life, and more importantly, that man had some good dick back in college, and that's something I hadn't had in a while.

Nasir called at about eleven a.m. on Thursday and told me that he would be in Houston at seven p.m. I couldn't even sit down the whole day; I was so happy and scared about seeing Nasir after six years. He knew I'd had a baby, and the day before, he had asked me how much I weighed. I had replied that I weighed 190 pounds. He coldly repeated, "190."

Nasir had been my first college fling, and it had been good and bad. That college fling had evolved into him introducing me to his family and us spending time together over Christmas break. Eventually I found out that the fucker had a "wifey" (main girlfriend) at home. I wouldn't take sloppy seconds from anyone, so I had to let him go (in college terms, I had to stop fucking him). You may wonder how he remained so special outside of great fucking sessions.

When I had found out that I was just the other bitch, I was crushed and angry. I had gotten into this man, and I was just another bitch he was passing time with. I let the drama queen out on his ass. I would cry, curse him out—*mind you, he had graduated and moved back home*— and have him come up to the school just to shut the door in his face. With all the bullshit I was trying to put him through for hurting me, all he kept saying was "I never even knew you had feelings for me. There is nothing I can say to ease your pain, but I'm going to keep coming and

answering your calls until you get over this."
And he did just that. He wasn't shit as my so-
called man, but he showed himself to be a good
friend, so that's why he held a special place with
me.

Damn, he looked shorter than I
remembered when I saw him. There was no real
vibe, but I was looking forward to the same good
sex, just like in our college days. I hoped he
didn't think that I just wanted to look at him all
night. After all the reunion bullshit, it was time to
take it down. There was still no chemistry, but I
wanted to fuck, so I went ahead and got me
some dick. It was trash. Nasir had the game
fucked up. He must have thought he was coming
to give a college girl some; hell, I was a grown
woman. In his defense, maybe he didn't like the
bigger version of me, but if that was the case, he
should have kept that weak performance in his
hand.

To add insult to an unsatisfied lover, the
dickhead had me help locate a so-called high
school mate who also lived in Houston. I took him
to visit while I went to a happy hour; I was
supposed to pick him up later.

Well, later turned into me waking up about
two a.m. He must have thought I was Boo-Boo
the fucking fool, so the drama queen in me had
to come out again. I called his cell and the house

he was at. Finally, at three a.m., I packed all his shit that was in my house and threw it on the porch of the house I had dropped him off at, after ringing the bell with no answer. The story ended with him staying at a hotel for the remainder of his stay and him concluding that I must be really hurt from my baby daddy to be wilding on his ass. My conclusion was that I was wasting my time for some weak dick that should have stayed a great college memory.

Use Your Madness to Make Money

I had moved to the Houston area because there had been a big hype over a huge attrition of teachers in Texas due to retirement that year, so I just assumed that securing a position would not be an issue. I had completed two internships in grad school, was shadowing a teacher in a local Texas district school, and was networking within various school districts. With all of that, I was still not receiving any potential job offers or even an interview.

Finally, I was called for a prescreening interview, and I found out that I would need an acceptance letter from my teacher's certification program stating that they had approved me as a certifiable computer teacher; then I would be able to get a second interview for a teaching position. I waited an hour for the program coordinator of the teaching program to meet with me about approving my paperwork.

When she rushed out of her office, she rudely told me that she had to go to her second job and that I would need to make another appointment.

My appointment for a second interview was the next morning, so being a baby mama who wouldn't take no for an answer, I hopped in my car and followed the program coordinator to her second job and waited in the hallway outside of the class she was teaching. I waited for three hours with my education portfolio and a binder of work samples. Since I was on a hunt for a job, I always made sure to keep all of my work samples and my portfolio in the car to ensure I would be prepared at any time an opportunity came up. When the first student walked out of class at nine o'clock, I rushed in. For the next ten minutes, I talked my ass off until she signed the necessary paperwork for me to take to my interview in   the   morning.

The Second Time Around

"Follow your heart, and it
will lead the way to your
true spirit."
                    -Unknown

My Own Memoirs...

Before you began to read the following section of this book I would like to challenge you review the questions below and get your **Mind Set** for the section...

1. Can you recall a time when you did something foolish twice?

    a. _____
    _____
    _____
    _____
    _____
    _____
    _____
    _____
    _____
    _____
    _____
    _____
    _____
    _____
    _____
    _____
    _____
    _____
    _____
    _____

Baby Mama Memoirs

August 5, 2005

When I read the quote on the front of the journal—"Follow your heart, and it will lead the way to your true spirit"—I bought this journal from the Dollar Store. I promised that I was going to write about where my heart had led me (in dealing with men) from my sperm donor JoJo to my first fuck Antonio; to my childhood-friend-turned-summer-fling Peter; to my college homie lover friend Nasir; to the thin line I walked between love and hate with my college boyfriend Cyrus; to my sterile baby daddy Raheem; then there was "The Magic Man" Jackson.

I decided to write about my relationships as a way to reflect on and learn from past errors: to hopefully be able to experience the true love of being touched, held, kissed, and truly safe with a man. The only problem was that I really didn't know what the standards and qualifications were that comprised a responsible and decent man.

Mommy Making It Happen

I wore a brown and tan striped suit (that didn't compliment my skin tone) to my second interview. I spoke in a fake broken foreign accent through an interview that lasted over two hours *and* I got that job. My two-bedroom, two-bathroom apartment in Texas was in an area that was all right, and I was prepared for my son to return in a few weeks. I'll never forget. It was August 10, 2004.

I had my Afro out and was wearing some black dress slacks and a white button-down with the school's logo. I walked into my neighborhood Kroger's grocery store and bumped into a coworker I had just met while sitting together at a teacher in-service. As we made some small talk, I noticed that she was in company with a quiet, sexy, older gentleman.

"Is that your man?" I asked simply. "Cause he is sexy as hell."

"No," she said. She went on to say that, "after our earlier conversation at the in-service," she didn't think "he would be my type."

Remembering our conversation, I asked if he was married or had children, because those were my two no-no's. The gentleman joined the conversation and said, "I have children, I take care of them and I can take care of you too."

I don't know if he was calling my bluff or if I was calling his. I explained that I had come into the grocery store for dinner, but since he had so much mouth, I said I'd had a change of plans: he would be treating me to dinner that night.

I took my coworker's number and address, got in my car, and went to dinner. We talked over dinner, and I talked as we toured the city. Hindsight showed me I gave him enough information for him to make himself into what I said I wanted. That was the day I met Jackson, who was fourteen years my senior.

He was from Chicago and was just in town visiting
his brother and sister-in-law, who had just relocated
for   her   position   as   a   teacher

It's My Turn

I was enjoying Jackson. Even though he had kids, he seemed to be a good single father. He had sole custody of his girls, and the others were grown. The relationship was moving fast, but when you have a good thing, you just enjoy the ride. We were about four months into this long-distance relationship when Jackson flew my son and I to Florida, so he could meet my child for the first time and I could meet his family at one of their church events. I wasn't big on sitting in church with his pastor mommy and daddy; I knew I was there to get my regularly scheduled bedroom time.

In the weeks that followed, I enjoyed flights to his hometown of Chicago, fine dining, and shopping trips. During my visits, I fell in love with Chicago. It was kind of like home. My research proved that a move to Chicago would mean a pay increase and much shorter travel to New Jersey (versus traveling from Texas). I also hoped I would be able to pursue my PhD at the local university.

My girl Andi constantly warned me that "A relationship that exists mainly on the phone, only truly exists in your head," but I turned my attention to my other friends and mentors who told me what I wanted to hear. Anyway, it was my turn.

Real Estate Realities

Jackson had informed me that he had left a city job that he had worked at for the past twenty years and that he was just rehabilitating investment properties full-time. Over the previous ten years, Jackson had owned several properties throughout Chicago and had some profits and losses on the books. I had always envisioned myself as a homeowner and landlord, and I became devoted in my research of home ownership and investment properties. Our common interest in investment property made our somewhat half-assed relationship into a business partnership.

I know what you're thinking: money and your man don't mix. But I would have sworn that this would be a surefire thing simply because Jackson already owned the property. He had also invested the last of his savings into the project. Therefore, I figured his investment in the success of the property would be imperative to his future. Plus, we also had a legal agreement between us regarding splitting the investment and future profits just in case our personal relationship didn't last.

What Do the Lonely Do at Christmas?

December 27, 2004

To celebrate our first Christmas together, Jackson bought me my first Mink. I wasn't that impressed, because I didn't know much about furs, and being that I lived in hot Houston, Texas, I really didn't see the point. Jackson also flew my son and me to Chicago for the week.

The biggest shock came with Jackson breaking up with me on Christmas night. He said that I was selfish, immature, and phony. First, we got into it at his niece's house when I noticed that he had bought all the children a wrapped gift and had given them five dollars each. Well, he didn't give my son a gift, and he overlooked DJ when he was passing out the five-dollar bills to all the kids in the house. I immediately confronted him about why my son didn't have a wrapped gift at the damned Christmas party that I hadn't known we were going to in the first place. He called me immature and referred to our agreement to go shopping in Chicago during the upcoming week. Understand that I had previously informed him that Christmas hadn't been a big deal in the past, because it had just been DJ and me, so I guess that came across as me not really being into the whole Christmas spirit.

My first Christmas as a mother, my baby was eight days old, and we spent it totally alone. That's the first time I heard the song "What Do the Lonely Do at

Christmas." Well, all I did that Christmas was cry and promise myself that I was going to avoid getting caught up in the special family moments, gift sharing, and the whole Christmas spirit.

For our next Christmas, DJ's paternal grandma bought him a Christmas Avon outfit that read "My First Christmas." It should have read "My First Christmas Being Claimed by You All." That Christmas, DJ went with his paternal grandma to a family Christmas dinner. I was informed that it wouldn't be a problem if I wanted to come with the baby. *Hell no,* I thought.

They were having a family dinner, and the only person in my house who was related to them was my son. At that time, I wasn't talking to, looking at, or fucking Raheem, so I wasn't going to be that baby mama who wanted to dress her child up and layer herself in a new sexy outfit just to get the attention of the motherfucker who had fucked me over and left me with our child. However, I did let my son go spend time with his family and I hoped he would enjoy the moment. I had cried for his first Christmas, so for the next one, I went to the club and partied. So went the stories of those sorry-ass years, one and two, but I thought year three should have been a charmer.

That Christmas was supposed to be special for the first time since I had become a mother. I was looking forward to the holiday season. I felt very comfortable and natural being with my son and Jackson, and I thought we would enjoy the holiday season as a family affair. A few weeks earlier, Jackson had asked me what I wanted for Christmas, and that was a question that I had never had to think about because the combination of a man, the holiday season, and me was somewhat like a pipe dream. Jackson may have been right that DJ wouldn't understand or remember that he hadn't gotten a Spiderman web glove like all the other boys had that night; but as a parent, it was my job to try to protect him from things he was too young to understand. That was a feeling that I knew too well.

Throughout my pregnancy and into my child's first two years, I had felt that I was purposely excluded from traditional routines and memories that I should have shared with my own family. Then I saw my child being treated in the same manner by someone I had invited into our lives. Hell no! Little did he know he was about to meet the monster in mommy.

Major Move

Most men are lying their asses off when they say they want independent women. They may love the thought of strong, aggressive, go-getters in the bedroom or when it comes to picking up the tab, but when they realize that the mind-set doesn't turn off for their fragile egos, their bullshit comes to light.

Over the next few months, the excitement of our half-assed relationship started to die—the sex was becoming infrequent and weak—and because I had become familiar with the Chicago life, I decided it would still be in my best interests for my career and business ventures for me to be able to monitor the progress of my investment property for myself. I made that decision without any discussion with Jackson, and by the time I had informed him, I had already secured four job offers, applied to graduate school, and was working on securing a two-bedroom apartment. I'd never had any intentions of living with a man, because as a single mother of just one, my routine revolved around just DJ and I.

Once I informed Jackson of my plans he insisted that it would be foolish to pay someone else's rent when I had invested in a gray stone building with three apartments and could live in one while the others were being worked on, so I agreed to his logic. I cancelled my rental agreement, and I postponed my move for a month so the workers could finish my apartment.

Everything was going great. My son had gone to his dad's for the summer. I had gone on my "Teachers Gone Wild" Bahamas vacation. I had verbally accepted a job offer that paid sufficiently better than the position I was leaving. I had an ownership interest in some investment property in a great location, and all I had left to do was unpack. The time had finally come for me to move to Chi-Town.

At about ten a.m., I pulled up to our property to see a crew working and when I walked in, my heart dropped.

Supposedly the property was being worked on for the past six months, but it looked like a damn shell with some drywall up and materials all over the place. Jackson proudly came up to me, bragging about his bullshit work.

At that moment, a part of me knew that I had fucked up and was dealing with a bullshit artist, so after voicing my concerns, I went to a hotel for a couple of days to work out an escape plan. Unlike my other relationships when I could just say, "fuck you," and keep it moving, I was committed to the relationship via my thirty-year mortgage, and my credit was the line. So I went back to try to work my way out of our bullshit arrangement.

Since my son was scheduled to be back in two months, I went hard based on the half-assed living conditions where we all would have to stay in one of the three-bedroom apartments. I made a to-do list, called contractors and potential investment buyers, did some of the manual labor, and had to start using my credit cards to purchase materials to bring the building to marketable standards to be sold as quickly as possible.

Jackson stopped working and just chilled like shit was good. His defense was that I was too aggressive.

"I'd rather cut off my nose to spite my face than deal with a woman like you," he said.

In the meantime, he was buying swimming pools when the building's water wasn't fully functional.

My attitude was "Fuck some summer fun when you can't provide the basic necessities like a bubble bath for your child." Within two months, we had a couple of offers, but Jackson's greed sabotaged every deal. I even went so far as to agree for him to receive all the profits of the sale. My goal was just to clear my portion of the mortgage and keep my good credit status, but he was holding out for his illusory million-dollar deal.

Baby Mama Memoirs

August 16, 2005

I just turned twenty-eight years old. I had just relocated to Chicago, Illinois, about two months before with the goal of obtaining a higher-paying teaching position, learning about and having more input on my first investment deal, and once again experiencing the special completeness of a relationship that I thought Jackson and I shared when we first met.

Well, as of the 16th of August I have used all of my Sprint peak minutes to call my potential high school office staff and went downtown to the Chicago Public Schools board of education, because I was not yet officially hired due to an incorrect job position number.

For the last six weeks, I had been calling and doing pop-in visits like a baby mama with only one diaper left at nine o'clock at night.

As of my birthday, the issue still had not been resolved; that meant that I didn't technically have a job or any medical benefits to provide for my son and myself. My next goal was my first investment deal. Well, at the current time, I was in $150,000 of debt for my investment in a three-unit apartment building that didn't have running water in any of the building's seven bathrooms.

Jackson will go down in the record books as the first man I believed in enough to mix my money into the relationship. I was truly scared of the relationship, because I had really believed everything that my Magic Man promised he could do. Many times, I asked myself why I trusted that man so much, what he had done that was special enough to deserve my attention. From the get-go, he wasn't scared to try to prove his love and support for me. I remembered my son's day care calling to say that they were rushing him to the hospital because of a seizure on a Thursday; Friday morning, Jackson had flown in from Chicago to be with us. Hell, my child's own father didn't even answer the phone when I tried to call him. Jackson provided intimacy; a big dick, the sweet babies ... and he didn't seem intimidated by my educational accomplishments.

Well, it was August 16, 2005, and the truth be told, it was all bullshit that I had accepted into my life. Jackson not being scared was maybe because he was a retired Chicago pimp.

The last time I had experienced any real intimacy with him was on the morning of December 25, 2004, and he called himself holding out on the fucking like the trick or some bitch that was trying to get her nails re-filled. Last but not least, the special tones he used to say baby or sweetie were the same he used to talk to every bitch that called on his fucking prepaid phone.

It was August 16, 2005, and I was going to seek the courage and wisdom to change the things that I could and ask the Lord to accept the things that I could or better yet, would not focus on in my life.

The next day I was back at my high school in the morning to see what the status was on my job.

Cut Straight to the Shit

The job's paperwork had been processed for me to start work, and my son came back from summer vacation, but my investment property was still in disarray. After about three weeks of the new routine, I was ready to throw my hands up. Then I received word from human resources that there were more issues with my position, so I used that as my sign to get the hell out of dodge—fuck my first home; fuck the job; and fuck that old fucking con artist. My son and I were out of there.

Within a week, I had found another position down south and an apartment. I packed our things in a U-Haul and left. Before I could even start my new job, my criminal record came back to haunt me, and even though I had reported it on my state application, the auditor said I should skip the question on the local application. I could see everything falling apart in front of my eyes. It seemed like I was watching a dramatic scene from a Lifetime   movie   in   slow   motion.

For the next two months, I depleted my savings and decided I had to go back to Chicago—not because of the man but for the mortgage I had signed. I didn't want to have to ask Jackson for any help with my son while I was planning to work long hours at the new position in Chicago, so before I returned, I dropped my son off with his father for an early Thanksgiving and Christmas break.

Baby Mama Memoirs
December 22, 2005

Three days before Christmas, DJ was with his father in Arkansas, and I was in Chicago at the building with Jackson and his two girls. We were all in one room, chilling and watching *Without a Trace*.

I really just wanted to talk to Jackson. I mentioned that DJ and I needed to take some family pictures because we hadn't taken any the year before. Then I asked if he and his girls took family pictures. He said yes, so I said that I had never seen them: "Where are they at?" He responded, "They're where they are supposed to be" in his leave-me-the-fuck-alone manner. It made me get up and go into my room alone. My effort to make small talk about some bullshit pictures at a point where everything is falling apart is really depressing.

Fuck it. It proved that I still wanted him and that I was still holding on to hope that things could get better, especially with the investment property.

Let's get back to Jackson. He would go down in the books as the first man I thought I was in love with as a grown woman and one of the very first men I trusted.

With that said, he would join the others—like my father—who proved to me that I could lie to myself about the love thing or just adapt to the image of the strong black women who were still alone.

When I met Jackson, it was supposed to be my first hit-and-run; yeah, I wanted him to be my first one-night stand. But we clicked. My son was away for the first time (with his father for the summer), and I had just moved to Texas and landed my first teaching job after about two and half months of searching.

Over dinner, I had told Jackson the truth about what I was feeling. You see, I talk a lot, and I could hold an interesting conversation about education, culture, sex, current events, etc., but not about how I felt or what was going through my head? I always figured who gave a fuck, but I felt certain easiness with Jackson. I told him about how bitter I was at having been left alone to raise and provide for my son and how scared I was about my move and new career/job.

It was really sad that I had to write my feelings in a damn book because I knew the one person I had thought really wanted to know everything about me was too busy watching fucking TV or waiting for the next dumb bitch he could use, to call. Jackson started trying to play the mental bullshit by saying, "You're not the prettiest thing, but neither am I." That's how I knew that the old asshole had never loved me, because his statement came across like he was saying that he was making an exception to his standards with me. Please, I was Ms. KIA. I saw him as the most beautiful man in the world. I loved his gray hair. I loved being with him whether he was dressed up or in his dirty work clothes. I was proud to be with him, because I thought I loved him and that he loved me. The man I was with was my standard of the best man. Obviously, you can see the difference in our views of each other.

Before I Let Go

That bullshit relationship was done, and as for my investment property, the consultant job wouldn't even begin to cover my basic living cost, let alone catch up on a late mortgage payment. With that said, Jackson and I had a truce and a long weekend just talking, laughing, and getting closure. That wasn't good enough for me. Oh no, I wanted to leave with a bang. Literally, I wanted to bang. You know how some people always have to have that last word? Well, it's something like that for me too, but instead of needing the last word, I needed the last fuck. The whole mission of this last fuck was to remind him why my name is Ms. KIA and to show him what he couldn't handle. I showed him. When I got off of him, I looked back down to see him curled up in a fetal position and shivering in the corner. Just the mere vision brought a smirk to my face. At the time, little did I know that what left him shivering had left me with a seed.

Maybe Baby

I spent Christmas day with Jackson's family at his aunt's house, and when the morning came, we hugged. I kissed him on the cheek and wished him and the house farewell. Then I picked up my child in Arkansas and headed back to Texas. That seemed like the most logical choice. I already had all of my teaching certifications there, so I assumed it would be easy to get a job. I called ahead and asked my brother if I could stay with him for a few weeks or a month, while I looked for a job.

Within days of arriving at my brother's house, I could tell shit wasn't right. Our older brother, who had a known drug problem, was not working, but staying at the house. There was no food in the refrigerator. The final clue came when I noticed that my brother slept with his bedroom door locked. As I searched for a job and things were unfolding at my brother's house, two dollar-store pregnancy test confirmed that I was pregnant.

When I told my friends, they were supportive, but they were against me having a second child.

My "promise pot" had about $420. *The "promise pot" is filled with money donated by close friends and family for a girl to get an abortion without having to deal with the asshole who got her pregnant.*

I already knew what it was like to have a baby alone from my first son, and like most single mamas, I promised I was not going to have another child until I was married or some shit like that. When I called and told Jackson about my pregnancy, he made himself clear: "Kill the baby, or I'll kill your credit." Yeah, he went straight for the jugular. (He knew I prided myself on having a good credit rating.) I was speechless. I just hung up the phone, and I knew exactly what I would be in for if I kept that baby. I really wanted to be wrong, but there was no question about how I felt about the baby.

In the midst of all this, I stopped my job search to care for my dying brother and help him plan his funeral and last wishes.

As a part of a stereotypical poor ass family, we had to prepare for some family members to show up and try to pull the power card.

Therefore, my brother's request was for me to get his house in order and take any heat from the family so that his son wouldn't have to deal with it; basically, I was to handle his dirty work and stand against the family. *I eagerly accepted.* My brother privately named me his power of attorney and executrix of his estate. I was looking for anything to avoid thinking about or dealing with the new pregnancy and no one outside of my "promise pot" circle knew about it.

My brother's health began to deteriorate quickly, so when he was admitted to the hospital, he made his first request of me. That request was that I get our older drug-addicted brother out of his house, and that would draw a line in the sand between me and the family; that would reestablish my outsider position in the family... oh well. I had the locks changed, told my brother he had three days to get his shit, and then I removed every item of his (from the bed to his clothes) and put them out for the Saturday trash pickup.

On February 26th, I told Jackson I was keeping my baby. Since he hated me for that we didn't need to continue to communicate; I suggested that he just sign over his parental rights so he wouldn't have any obligation to the child.

"Don't call me, and I won't call you" were Jackson's exact words. He went on to fix his mouth to say, "I didn't want a baby by a black, nappy-headed bitch, so kill the baby, and I never want to see you again." For weeks, he didn't call, and I began to accept that I was in the situation alone.

At first, I couldn't pull it together, even though I didn't talk about it: People could see the hurt and sadness in my face, in my uncoordinated outfits, and in my dry conversation.

Then I did the bitter and lonely woman makeover; I cut off all my hair, threw away all the old clothes I had worn while dating Jackson, and stayed busy away from home and by myself. Well, the haircut had to be redone and dyed and then completely cut off. I knew that new hair-do was going to have me looking like a little potbellied boy in a few weeks.

If Mommy Could See Me Now

My brother passed, and I couldn't even grieve, because I had to keep my guard up to deal with all of my family's bullshit. In 1998, I had experienced the death of a close family member for the first time. I had come in from college to attend the evening hours of the viewing service.

My mother had stood up in front of the church and said, "I ain't going to say no names, but I've got a daughter who goes to college and is so educated that she's too good to speak to me. She walked away, but she'll have to crawl back."

After one of my aunts had told me what my mother said, I caught up to her as she was getting into her brother's van and I told her off, saying, "What the fuck? Your sister is dead, and it's not always about your ass. You're not saying any names ... hell, I'm the only bitch in your whore ass family who has ever been to or looked at a damn college!"

Most normal families share a sense of pride and joy in each other's accomplishments; that's not true in a dysfunctional family.

Shirley Caesar had a song that I used to sing when I was little called "Living in the Last Days" (a time when people called wrong *right,* when mothers were against their daughters and fathers were against their sons). That song truly describes my family's dynamics.

The last time my mother and I had been face-to-face had been right before my brother's funeral. She had asked me if I wanted a piece of her.

A bit shocked by my mother's bold threat, I said, "I have too much class to beat you like you used to beat your mother."

That verbal argument started when my mother started talking to her sister in Dallas on the phone. My mother was always sure to remind me that I was nothing but an educated dummy and that I was the same crazy little girl she used to get a check for. She said she still should be getting a check for raising me.

The argument also covered how my degrees didn't mean anything. She said they must have been giving them away for me to get them.

No matter how much I thought I was "All of That," she said, "you'll always be a welfare, jailhouse, baby mama".

I know some might say, "That's so sad"; "That's cruel"; "You poor baby." I say that, if you are going to be beaten, be beaten by the best.

Between my mother, my oldest brother, and my other close family members, I had been called every kind of black, dumb, crazy whore or bitch in the book. At that time, no one knew I was about three months pregnant. I went through my entire pregnancy alone. I was already in a different state, and I only told three family members (Aana, Aunt Addison, and Aunt Rose in New Jersey) about the baby. No one in my immediate family knew about my second son until I texted my brother a picture of him.

When I was younger, I was sad and confused about the way I felt I was treated and viewed by my family. Then I finally said, "Fuck it. No matter how good or bad I am, I will never be shit to this fucked-up family."

I became numb, and I tried to use that numbness to my advantage when I started my educational escape. I was able to tune out bullshit from college peers, professors, or even supervisors & bosses trying to insult me or break my spirit. After the family abuse, I didn't have any more room for scars that anyone else   might   want   to   inflict.

Crying and Calling

April 9, 2006

I promised myself that I wasn't going to do that bullshit again, but there I was crying and calling again.

Then it happened. I had already known it was coming on Tuesday, April 4, 2006. I had woken up that morning to a weird dream that I was taking Jackson's two daughters to summer camp in Texas where I was currently living. Well, at 2:19 p.m. on that Tuesday afternoon, I noticed a missed call from Jackson. Missed calls were how we used to communicate, because he only had a prepaid cell phone with limited minutes. So he would call and let it ring for my caller ID to pick up his number. Then he would wait for me to return his call at night when he had free incoming calls (after nine p.m.).

I'm not going to front. I was happy as hell to see his number appear on my phone. My heart wanted to believe that he might be calling to check on the baby and me. But in reality, he was just calling for some bank information in an effort to sell our pre-foreclosed building. We spoke for a hot minute regarding the building updates, and after that, I informed him of the upcoming insurance bill that was due on Friday, which he had said he would pay. On Saturday, his prepaid cell was turned off until he got more minutes, so I was unable to reach him to confirm if he had made the insurance payment for our investment property.

When I finally spoke to him, he hadn't kept his word, as usual, and he promised to handle the bill on Monday.

In the Meantime & Between Time

One Friday, I received a letter from the state workforce office notifying me that I hadn't been approved for unemployment benefits because my previous job said that I had abandoned my position.

To top it off, my friend Monica, whom I had asked to help move my brother's old, heavy couch outside for the second week in a row didn't show up or call. So my four-and-a-half-month pregnant ass moved the couch by myself. On Saturday, she called at eight forty-five a.m. I kept it short and opted not to fuck with her right then.

Afterward, I wanted to stop crying, but I couldn't. Every time I went to the mailbox and saw the letter from foreclosure lawyers, every time I started cleaning to make my brother's house homely, I got so lonely.

Every time I looked at my son who was sleeping hard after another long day of running around with me just reminded me how much

I had fucked up my life. I was trying not to think about it.

In the morning, I went to the work-source employment office and spent three to five hours looking for any type of employment, or to the park to read, or did anything to stay around people so I could put on a front of not dwelling on the bullshit in my life.

I hadn't received a callback from a job in five months. I was having my second child by an asshole that had told me to kill the baby and that he never wanted to see me again. To top it all off, my first home was in foreclosure, and I was in debt for more than two hundred thousand dollars.

Yep, two hundred thousand dollars, and I didn't have a damn thing to show for it, because unlike my asshole of a business partner, I had used the damn money for the investment! You never know how low and dirty someone really is until it's too late to get out of the bullshit.

Baby Mama Memoirs

April 15, 2006

I talked to and argued with Jackson for about an hour today. I called because I was upset about the building being in foreclosure, my late property insurance, and the reason we had a fucked-up relationship. His side seemed logical, and I could agree with and understand a lot of his bullshit points of view. However, since my position was more emotionally charged, he concluded that I was the crazy one in the relationship.

I wished I had a Dr. Phil to talk to, because I didn't understand why I couldn't seem to secure a healthy intimate relationship and good communication with my selected male partner. I knew that part of it had to do with my issues with my own relationship or lack of a relationship with my father.

Damn it, I was grown and I should have been over that bullshit, but when I thought about my father, I still got those fucked-up feelings.

April 23, 2006

Be Thankful	
Pros	Cons
I lived in a house with running water DJ had his own room I had food to eat I had a washer and dryer accessible I had a TV and cable My cell phone was on I had a radio The baby was okay so far DJ was behaving in school	My first home was in foreclosure I was past due on my credit cards My unemployment benefits had not cleared

Goals	
For Right Now	For the Near Future
Get a teaching job for the school year and a summer position at the YMCA Don't mess with or call Jackson Smile and enjoy the next four and a half months of pregnancy Retake the GRE Pay off: • Mom's insurance • Children's Place credit card • Exxon credit card • Chase credit card • car insurance • car maintenance repair Fix the negative balance in my checking account	Have a home of my own for my family Find a great career job Go back to college for a PhD program Build my kids' savings accounts and get them whole-life insurance Learn to communicate in an intimate relationship

May 25, 2006

On Mother's Day, I called and cursed Jackson out. I hung up on him; in return he hung up on me. I called and cursed out his answering machine until his cell phone couldn't receive any more messages. I called Jackson all kinds of names—bitch, coward—and even talked about his kids and how poorly his parents had raised him. (Most likely his stubborn, Gemini ass wasn't bothered by the messages.) Maybe he didn't even listen to them.

May 31, 2006

My six-month checkup would be soon. Damn. In three months, I was going to be the single mother of two little boys.

I was proud to say that I had been clean for two weeks—clean not from drugs or alcohol... but from cursing a motherfucker out.

I had always wondered why or how a woman could become a single mother with a second and third child. Having my first child alone had been a hard pill to swallow, and I had promised myself that I would never go through that again. You hear that shit everywhere: "I'm not having another child until I get married."

Like that really makes a difference when someone doesn't give a fuck about you; as a disclaimer you can say "At least I'm married" or "At least my kids all have the same daddy." Never say never!

Look, I wanted my first child to be acknowledged and accepted by his father so badly that I moved from my home state of New Jersey, where all of my friends and family were, and went back to Arkansas to have my first child there, just to give the father the opportunity to take part in his life. I did so also to prove beyond a shadow of a doubt to him and myself that he was the father. When I didn't think it could get any worse, it did with baby daddy number two. Well, I'm gonna say "Never," I want my tubes tied....hell they can pull the pussy out cause I don't want to go through that shit again.

It's A Good Day

Baby Mama Memoirs
July 13, 2006

For the last few weeks, I had been crying to the point of giving myself headaches; this amounted to far too many days of inactivity. About July 11th I received a call from a potential buyer for my pre-foreclosure home in Chicago. The man said that he had been trying to reach Jackson but that his number wasn't in service and he only had five days to get Jackson's signature before his offer would be void. I had spoken to Jackson a few weeks before, and he had told me that he had moved from Chicago and that his phone would be disconnected on the seventh of that month. Well, up until that point, I hadn't thought about him not having, or better yet me not having, a number to contact him. But to relay the buyer's message, I called Jackson's sister and his son and told them to call him and tell him that the man in Chicago needed to speak to him ASAP. The next day, the potential buyer informed me that he had gone to the building. Jackson's daughters were there, and they had given him Jackson's new number, which he, in turn, gave to me. He had a Nextel phone with an Atlanta number; I took the number for future reference.

So I went about my business as usual. As I sat on the corner of my bed, I looked in the mirror and thought to myself, *He didn't love me. He didn't try to help me. He doesn't care about my child. He's with and doing for the person he cares about, and even though it hurts like hell to be alone and carrying his child, I'm still making it. I'd rather be alone than with someone who doesn't appreciate what I have to offer.

As soon as I finished that thought, the shit hit the fan. First, the buyer called and informed me that he had spoken to Jackson; he was in Georgia and would be back on Sunday. Then I spoke with Jackson's sister, and she informed me that she had also spoken to Jackson.

He had told her to make sure that she didn't give me his new number, because I was trying to set him up. A few hours later, Jackson's son also informed me that his dad had said not to give me his number, and I started to flip out. I told his son to tell his dad that I already had his number, that I didn't need to call around to get shit, and that I had never called him about my fucking kids or their damn needs, because I was a fucking mother who knew how to take care of my kids' needs.

I hung up the phone and started to call to leave him a message about his punk ass, but when I went to pick up my phone, my eyes fell on my open closet. All I saw were the hanging clothes at size zero months to 3T, another bag full of baby clothes, and my shoe rack with five pairs of shoes that were sized between two and six. I thought to myself *I'm doing what I have to do to prepare for this baby, and if I really believed that he cared or was going to help, I wouldn't have prepared myself to do it alone. So why call and leave him a message when I'm already handling business.*

This whole second time around had been hard for me to accept mentally, physically, and emotionally. The mere thought of recalling the man I had thought I loved, telling me that he wanted the baby

I was carrying to be aborted and not to call him again had me crying daily, losing my hair, and even losing weight during the pregnancy. But I was still able to buy the baby's clothes, a stroller, a car seat, a swing, a playpen, and a cabinet full of baby food/water, and none of that had been a gift from a baby shower. When I reflected on my situation like that, I didn't feel the need to beg for his attention or affection by calling his new number.

The dumb fucker must have forgotten that I was Ms. KIA and that I had the most important number—his social security number and his parents' address. With that said, it was a good day. *That* day, I was able to utilize "mind over matter"—if you don't mind, it doesn't matter.

It's Sunday Again; Paint the Pain Away

Baby Mama Memoirs
July 16, 2006

Since I knew that Sundays tended to be sad days for me, I planned to try and redirect my sorrow into something more productive. First, I set the alarm on my cell for 7:20 a.m. and 4:20 p.m. so I could remember Joel Osteen in the morning and T.D. Jakes in the evening. On Saturday, I had visited Home Depot, Big Lots, and Wal-Mart to price and purchase concrete caulking to seal some cracks in the house's foundation and to get some paint to finish the last of the three bedrooms.

I only caught half of Joel Osteen and I planned to do some outside housework. However, when I loaded the caulk gun, the tube burst on the wrong end. I was in the process of getting dressed to go exchange the caulking when my mind started drifting again. I began to wonder and start imagining that it would be so much better if Jackson were here to show me how and to help me repair the house since I only had about six weeks to get ready before baby Dylan would arrive. In the meantime, my four-year old son's lack of activity resulted in him disturbing me. What really made me sad was when DJ and I were shopping in Wal-Mart and he said, "Mommy, you don't have to buy new stuff, because I'll go to Jackson's house and get your stuff and beat him up, 'cause I'm big now." I told him that was okay and explained that Jackson was not my friend anymore. I said we'd get new and better stuff for our new house. I knew that some of my son's comments had come from what he may have overheard me say on the phone.

I believed that my child had some understanding of the difference in his mommy not having her own things, since it had always been him and I doing everything together—from window-shopping to comparing prices to actually buying items for our home and for our basic necessities. Even though I had held onto some of my son's personal items, most of my stuff and stuff for the house was gone.

So instead of dwelling on my child comments we went and got some Mickey D's. Then we ate dinner together, watched cartoons for a half-hour, and took a nap. I went to sleep and hoped I would feel better when I woke up. When I got up, I still felt a little sad, so I decided to try to work through it instead of just sitting and crying. It was about nine p.m., so I decided to just paint the borders and edges of the room. When I started painting, I tried to hide my face from my son so he wouldn't see the tears running down my face again. But you know how nosey little kids are.

"Why are you crying again, Mommy?" he asked.

I explained to him that Mommy was sad and that I was crying so I could let the sad feelings out so I could feel better later. Painting through the pain helped to keep my mind off of some of my life's mess.

I'm Going to Tell Your Mama

My childhood, especially my situation with Shay, had already shown me that grand-mamas were going to have their sons back no matter how sorry their sons were, but I decided to call Jackson's mother anyway. I had met Jackson's mother numerous times, and she was very sweet and loving to my first son. Plus, Jackson's parents were church preachers. She answered the phone, and we exchanged our greetings. Then the conversation went on.

"Just wanted you to know that I'm scheduled to have the baby on September 6th," I said.

"Oh, you're having a baby? By whom?" his mother asked.

"Your son, Jackson."

"My son was here all weekend, and he didn't mention anything about having a baby."

"We are no longer dating, and he's moving on with his life, but I wanted to inform you about your grandchild," I told her.

"Look, I have plenty of grandchildren," she said. "There ain't nothing special about the one you're carrying."

"I don't need anything from anybody. I just thought you would want to know."

"Baby, you should pray that God sends Jackson back to you," she said.

"No," I said. "I'm going to pray that God blesses me with a job to take care of my family. Well, I have to go. Goodnight."

Baby Mama Memoirs

July 23, 2006

Joel Osteen spoke about the power of remembering. He said to remember what God had already done and to recall the good things God once had done because he could do it again. Instead of complaining, he said we should go back and remember all the Red Seas that God had parted for us. He said to start dwelling on our victories and not focusing on the problems that were depressing us.

T.D. Jakes spoke about the frustration of liberation and of being stuck in the wilderness. I was tired of going off and having to apologize. He said to untie my joy, my finances, and my mind. He said it would take a while to get free.

One Week and Counting

Baby Mama Memoirs
August 29, 2006

I was scheduled to have a C-section on the first Wednesday of September, but I wished I would go into labor. I was so ready to get the pregnancy over with it. This pregnancy seemed longer and lonelier than the first. I was scared as hell, because once again i didn't have a plan or a job. The fear and hurt built up for a few nights and I walked the floors crying until I got so weak and tired I passed out on the couch listening to an oldies/R&B station on the radio.

I had to get my bullshit out my heart and head, and the best way a baby mama could do that (in my case) was by calling and cursing out the asshole that had hurt and left her. Well, I had a whole lot of choice words, but there was one problem—I had torn up his number after the last time I had called and cussed him out. I had promised myself not to call again. Hell, life had already proven to me that promises were made to be broken. I knew that my deadbeat baby daddy's son and other family members were not going to give me his number, so I called Chicago and told one of his former business associates that my bank needed a contact number to complete some paperwork before they could cut him a check. Of course, he gave it to me. Then it was on.

Important note: If you are going to be calling, crying, and cussing a motherfucker out, choose your words carefully, especially when the person is too cowardly to pick up the phone and leaves you to be taped on his machine. Make sure there is no mention of death, of hurting them, or of getting them, because that shit can get your ass put in jail. Between the crying and the cussing, be sure to clearly clarify why you are calling.

Mention any and all monies owed and the baby; just in case you have to prove just cause if/when you go to court.

Well, the first four or five messages were mostly cursing and mostly ended in crying, but in the sixth through the tenth message, you really get to the point of speaking understandable English. The best ones are messages eleven through thirteen, because you realize that he's not even going to listen, and if he did, it still wouldn't help your hurt. Finally, you end the call with the promise not to call again. Even though it seems pointless to others, the answer machine allowed me to get shit off my chest. I never really expected him to pick up the phone, but I kind of got off knowing that he was scared to pick up and hear my voice over the phone, even though I was in Texas and he was in Georgia. The fucked up thing about how I was feeling was that I was crying more about my credit score and the fact I had trusted him with the goal of getting my first home more than the fact that he had left me to live with some Section 8 bitch and left me a child to raise alone.

Delivery Time: The Baby's Birth with DJ First

My C-section was scheduled for noon on a Wednesday, so Monica and I reported to the hospital at ten thirty a.m., and Tauja met us in my assigned room. Before I could have the baby, I needed to make preparations for my firstborn. Being that it was only me and my baby, I had to depend on Monica to stay at my house and put DJ on the bus. She would go to school and come back to pick DJ up early from school and take him to work with her. Their day would end at my house for the evening. I only had fifty-five dollars of my final unemployment check, but I gave it to her for some gas. Monica did that favor for me on Wednesday, Thursday, and Friday. It was nice of my ex-coworker Tauja to take off of work to be with me at the hospital. Because of my family history, no one in my family (with the exception of Aunt Addison, Aana, and Aunt Rose) even knew I was having my second child or was even pregnant.

Monica came into the delivery room with me for my C-section. As I lay on the table, my mind started to reflect on the pain of once again being left alone for nine months with a child who was not wanted by the father.

My theme song started playing in my head: "I Was a Fool." I told myself, "No, no, no. It's not about you." There's so much that can happen to a child that I had no control over, so I just needed to pray that my nine months of pain and tears hadn't affected the health of my baby.

Then I started thinking, "I don't feel no ways tired; I've come too far from where I started from." I had been told, and I believed that we are our own worst enemies; the enemy was in me. With that said, the battle began in my head.

A part of me wanted to go and be in a place where I would be numb to the pain of the past and the present, like Mary J. Blige was in *Prison Song* when she was in the mental institution. The other part of me was telling me to suck it up—"You have a four-year-old and a new baby that only have you to take care of and love them."

First, I could hear Jackson's voice saying, "Kill that baby, and I don't want to see you again." Then I would hear the chorus line of the church song ("I don't believe he brought me this far"). Then I heard Jackson's voice, then the chorus line, then Jackson's voice, then the chorus line.

The anesthesiologist asked, "Are you okay?"

I just laid there with tears streaming down my face.

I could feel the pressure of the doctors pushing and pulling, but it didn't compare to the battle going on in my head. I had a headache and could barely keep my eyes open when Monica brought baby Dylan to me to look at. His birth time was 12:49 p.m., but I wasn't able to see him again until later that evening, because I was in recovery with the shakes, which had something to do with my blood pressure and sugar levels. Tauja stayed with me in the recovery room until I was taken to my room with the baby.

On my second day in the hospital, I received a call from a Florida number, and when I answered the call to hear Jackson's voice (during the last nine months, he had moved to three different states and changed his number just as many times... I guess to avoid me), he hesitantly said, "Hi. I just called to say thank you and, if you need anything, just call me."

"Okay," I said. "Bye."

I was released on Saturday, two hours later Monica brought DJ home with his new little brother and me.

Two-Week-Old

Dylan was two weeks old, and my body was feeling better. I was not planning to mow the lawn, so I tried to talk to my neighbors' landscapers and make an appointment to have the lawn cut and edged in the morning. The morning came and went; although it was an chore I preferred to avoid, I had to suck it up and cut the damn yard to avoid being fined by the neighborhood association.

What Can I Do?

Baby Mama Memoirs
September 25, 2006

Dear Lord,

I need to write to you, because maybe you can't hear my cries or maybe you're not looking in my direction to see my tears. But I have tried everything to be a good mother and provider for my children, and every time it seems like it's getting better, something fucked-up happens again. I promised myself that if you blessed this child, I wouldn't act like a crazy baby mama the second time around. I promised to just accept this situation for what it is, and I have been good since my second son was born. I haven't called Jackson cursing or trying to set some shit off. But I can't say it's because I'm trying to take the high road, because it might just be that I'm too damn tired to fight anymore. I have to live with the hurt, the shame, and the embarrassment of knowing that, when I told him about the baby, he told me that he didn't want a baby by a black, nappy-headed bitch. What am I supposed to do now that I have a newborn, no job, no childcare, and no help. What?

Call the fucker who caused the pain and who made it clear, by changing his number and moving to three different states, to see what part he plan to play in our life? Not this time around...

Closure After Being Kicked to the Curb

Baby Mama Memoirs
November 6, 2006

Patience is a virtue, and it paid off on November 6th. Jackson called and asked how it felt to be a welfare woman again. I told that motherfucker just how I felt within five minutes and *without* cursing or crying. Whether he was listening or even cared was not the point; what was important was what came out of my mouth and that I was a lady about it. Better yet, I was Aunt Addison. When I returned his call, the conversation began with me stumbling over my words and rambling, but after a few moments the words just started flowing. My words became so direct and clear that he wasn't able to interrupt me or refute my points. My objective was not to attack him; I just needed him to know that he had abandoned me and hurt me and that I was not just going to let him start calling me and acting like nothing had ever happened just because he had some curiosity about a kid he didn't want and had not seen. To answer his question, I simply said, "Everything that I've lost, I worked for, and I'm going to work to get it back."

Almost Made It a Month

Baby Mama Memoirs
October 1, 2006

On October 4th, Dylan would be four weeks old. It hit me the Sunday before, maybe because I had messed up my schedule. I always treated Sunday as the family day with Joel Osteen at seven thirty and T.D. Jakes at four thirty p.m. But that day, I missed T.D. Jakes at four thirty. Yeah, dumb-ass number two (Jackson) called and promised to send me twenty-five dollars for the baby, but how the fuck was he going to send that small amount of money when he didn't even have any of my information (like an address). I just listened to his bullshit without any emotion or attempted correction. He was back in Atlanta, Georgia, for the weekend, and that's where his sisters, daughters, and so-called friends were living. His "friend" had received more money from him than I had during my entire pregnancy and the first month of my child's life—which totals zero dollars and zero cents.

On top of the baby bullshit, a close friend informed me that a former administrator had told her that our previous boss was the reason I couldn't attain employment in the school district. That bitch used to brag about how she could blackball a person throughout the district, but I felt that once an administrator saw my service record, school participation, and evaluation rating of "Exceeds Exceptions," that would speak for itself. I used my jobs as my creative outlet; they were my only real outlets as a single mother. I prided myself on my ability to block out social stereotypes and build an environment in which I made only excellence my standard.

I did exactly that in my classroom, in afterschool clubs, and in any program activities that I participated in.

I worked with an attitude that allowed my students and me to enjoy being there. However, the flip side was intolerable to some. Maybe if I had hidden the fact that I was a single mother and if I had played the divorced card or the overseas husband card, I would have gotten by a little easier at that job. My first teaching position provided for my family so I didn't view myself as a baby mama just as a mother with a child.

At my first teaching job I would go in on Saturdays to do a little extra work, so I would bring my then two-year-old son with me while I installed software, graded papers, or made copies. On one particular Saturday, the principal called me into her office.

"Have a seat Ms. Swain," the principal said. "I would like to ask you about something I have noticed."

"Okay."

"Where is your son's father?"

"Home, I guess," I said.

"Where is home?"

"Arkansas."

"Did you love him?"

"I love my son."

"No. Do you love the man you made a child with?"

"I don't know how they did it in your day, but love is not a requirement in the baby-making process," I said. Then I exited the awkward conversation, letting her know that I had a play date with my son at Celebrity Station. Upon my exit, she offered me discount coupons for the kid zone, and we left it at that.

From that point on, she made it a point to have something sarcastic to say or to belittle me. Every time she would see me, she would look me in the face and check me from head to toe and then not speak when I smiled and said, "Good morning."

I don't know if her attitude was intended to make me mad or to degrade me, but because I was just coming off of welfare and onto a salary, there wasn't anything she could do to make me mad about my money.

She tried all kinds of bull.

Once I walked through the office in my black-and-white-striped suit and popping red heels. She decided to announce to the office, which was full of teachers and some parents, that she had hired "hootchies." I quickly responded with a smirk on my face, "You forgot to say fine hootchies" and proceeded to proudly sashay out of the office. I was called back to the office over the intercom system and given a twenty-minute lecture about how she had done it in her day. She said she was not jealous, just schooling me. To shut her up, I referred to her as the top diva, and then she excused me. Don't get me wrong, I made sure to always keep my large chest covered and to wear appropriate-length bottoms; who would have guessed that a Target wardrobe could make people so inflamed?

The bitch went so far as to release my son's private records about me seeking a speech pathologist about his speech issues, as a means to belittle me. During all her rude comments and petty attacks, I kept a silly smirk on my face, because even though I was a bit confused about her objective at that time, it didn't hinder my personal or professional performance. I believe she wanted a "professional head popper" (that is a hood chick that works in a professional setting but feels the need to maintain her classless ways to validate her hood credit) for her office entertainment. Hell no, if I wanted to act like a hoodrat I would have stayed in the hood, so the only show she got from me was the proficiency of a grown woman working.

Years later, I was feeling that bitch's effects. I really needed a job to feed my kids: I didn't have a choice or any resources, so I was going to have to take my bachelor's degree, my dual master's degrees, and my teacher certification down to the welfare office once again to ensure I would be able to give my children the basic necessity of food.

This welfare shit again—all because some bitch wanted to play with my financial security. I had to stop focusing on that bitch, though, and come up with a plan to get in and out of the welfare system as quickly as possible.

I really needed the childcare services to help me get on my feet again. Welfare was not set up to help you if you had a job, but if you were at home all day and not working, they would provide you with child care services. That seemed backward as hell, but oh   well.

The Battle between being a Bitter or Better Mama

I'm not what I was ten years ago
or ten minutes ago. I'm all of that
and then some. And whereas I
can't live inside yesterday's pain,
I can't live without it.

–George Wolf,
The Colored Museum

My Own Memoirs...

Before you began to read the following section of this book I would like to challenge you review the questions below and get your **Mind Set** for the section...

1. Do you know what depression is?
   a. Yes
   b. No

2. Have you ever been depress over a parent/child relationship?
   a. Yes
   b. No

3. If you are feeling sad, lonely, and/or confused who are the people you seek out for assistance or advice?
   a. Friends
   b. Family Members
   c. Self Help (books, mediations, etc.)
   d. Other _____

4. Do you believe single parents can successful raise a child alone?
   a. Yes
   b. No

5. What do you believe is the most important resource that a single parent needs to care for their family?
   a. _____

Letter to God

Dear God,

It's assumed that parents want to provide and do better for their children, but as we all know, there is no blueprint or step-by-step guide to ensure the success of your children. Based on my childhood experiences and my limited resources as a single mother of two, I truly didn't know where to start, but I know I wanted my boys to know that they have worth in this world. I wanted to set them up to be better prepared to make life choices. The road to recovery is still rough; I need to see a little light in my tunnel of trouble. God, I want to be better not bitter.

Everyone but Me Slept in a Bed

Baby Mama Memoirs
January 7, 2007

On January 6th, my boys and I were riding to the store to do a little Saturday shopping. Baby Dylan (who was four months old) was sucking his fingers, and DJ (who was five years old) was talking as usual. Watching *Super Nanny*, I had learned to take the time to be an active listener, so I kept the radio off and asked probing questions about whatever he was talking about.

Here's just a little background. After a whole year of not visiting or seeing his child, Mr. Dad-of-the-Year showed up on DJ's birthday to assert his court-ordered visitation rights, so in order for me to stay out of jail, I let him take DJ for a visit. We agreed that he would take him from December 17th through the 26th. Hell, it was only eight days; he shouldn't get tired of flossing and playing daddy that fast.

Well, DJ started talking about the night he stayed at his daddy's girlfriend house.

"Mommy, doggies sleep on the floor, and I sleep like a doggie."

"When were you a doggie?" I asked

"At daddy's girlfriend's house, I slept like a doggie on the floor," he said.

"Where did Raheem sleep?"

"In the bed with his girlfriend," he said. "He gave me a pillow, but she got mad, because she didn't want it on the floor."

"Where did her kid sleep?" I asked.

"She was in her bed," he said. "Everyone sleeps in beds, and my dad made me sleep on the floor."

I immediately called Raheem and asked him to explain what DJ was talking about.

"Just because y'all New Yorkers are all stuck up doesn't mean I'm going to raise him to be some big time New Yorker when he's down south," the dumb ass replied. "And down south, we sleep on floors."

"No, dumb ass. Y'all didn't sleep on floors! You, your bitch, and your bitch's kid, slept in beds. The only one on the floor was your child," I said. "I didn't call to argue with you. I just wanted to point out that once again, you managed to prove to your only child and your bitch of the week that you don't give a fuck about your damn child. One more thing... I'm from New Jersey, and New York and New Jersey are two different states, dumb ass. Good day, you sorry ass bitch."

With that, I hung up.

Mission 007

Baby Mama Memoirs
January 9, 2007

My theme for the year 2007 was "007 Mission: Mission of Making It." My children were five years old and four months old, and I had made sure that my baby-making phase would be done with. I would be the one attending the baby showers and wishing others well during their diaper days.

I just accepted a new job and the beginning of a new potential career move. I would be a GED instructor at the community college, and I would also be the TANF (Temporary Assistance for Needy Families) program coordinator consultant. Those two positions were both classified as part-time, but with the Lord's blessing of good health for my children and me, I planned to max the weekly hours and overtime to once again be able to provide for my home and future goals. I thought those two positions would be perfect opportunities to give me the needed experience to use my master's degrees and make me more marketable in my career endeavors.

Mother's Day 2007

The night before Mother's Day: My boys were washed, fed, and in the bed. It was approximately eleven thirty p.m. and I had called my aunt Addison in New Jersey to help me prepare some baked mac and cheese for the Mother's Day dinner I was planning for myself. After I finished getting her instructions, I decided to run a hot bath and attempt to relax my mind and body from the random thoughts of me being a baby mama who was struggling to be a single mother while my babies' daddies were spending their money buying new cars, spending weekends at casinos, and eating out at their leisure. As I sat there trying to fight those random thoughts the tears began falling down my face.

The Bullshit of Mother's Day 2007

On May 13, 2007 at 2:01 p.m., I received a text on my cell that read, "Happy Mother's Day and tell DJ I said hi." The fucking nerve of that baby daddy!

Just three weeks before, I had called, asked, explained-- hell, I even had the doctor fax Raheem the paperwork regarding our son's emergency dental problem. My baby was in pain and needed some teeth pulled and some filled. I used to carry private insurance for my child, and I never asked Raheem to contribute to court-ordered medical bills that was ordered. But I was just working two part-time jobs for the same institution, and those hours didn't provide medical benefits. However, the job provided just enough money to have me be denied state medical benefits for my children.

Well, back to the bullshit, I told Raheem about our son's daily pain and that I really needed him to step up and please help me because I just didn't have it.

He agreed, and the day I was scheduled to take DJ to the dentist I took off from my hourly paying job. I knew that he had a history of trying to set me up, so I let him deal directly with the dentist's office about the charges.

I gave him our son's saving account number and told him to put the money in before I went to have them start the dental procedure. A bitch will be a bitch. The asshole called and told me he was at the bank but that his new girlfriend and his mother had told him he should get a receipt first or have the actual doctor call him directly because I was just trying to get all his money.

As my son sat in the backseat of my car holding his jaw waiting to go the dentist, I just started crying and cursing him out. How dare he? He had never paid for any medical bills or coverage.

How could he think that $1400 could even begin to fix my financial problems?

Through some of my yelling and cursing I heard Smokie Norfield's, "You Been Good" playing on my car radio. I slammed the phone closed, pulled over in a shopping center parking lot, and just cried my heart out. What kind of mother couldn't help her own child in pain?

When all was said and done, I went and reapplied for Medicaid for the kids. After that, I went to the dollar store and bought three tubes of oral pain gel and called and rescheduled for the next available appointment for my baby. It would be six weeks later, and I hoped something would come through by that   time.

Quan's Graduation

Baby Mama Memoirs
June 2007

I should go. I shouldn't go. I should go. I shouldn't go ... go, stay, go, stay, go, stay—fuck it, I'm going, I thought. Airline tickets for a five-year-old look expensive as hell when you are broke and have to travel with two kids. Back in the day when I was a first-year teacher with one kid, it had been no big thing to plan a trip for my son and me. A nonstop Continental flight was about two hundred and fifty dollars each for a roundtrip ticket purchase a few weeks in advance. Add another child and subtract a little stable income from a teacher's salary, and you get five to eight-hour connecting flights with a $552 total. I had to ask myself if it made more sense to go to my nephew's graduation or to just send a card and call it a day. I really wanted to be there for my nephew Quan's special moments in life.

Since I had moved down south and had my own child, we had really started drifting apart. I guess it was expected with him growing into a young man. What wasn't expected was the asshole attitude that my nephew had toward me. I understood that he was still a kid and couldn't fully comprehend the financial struggles of being a single mother, but when I went to give him my gift of an inspirational book for college students, he pushed it back into my hands. He said he didn't want it, because I wouldn't let him borrow my rental truck as a better gift to ride to a graduation after-party. When I refused, he proudly let me know that, when he got his Bentley, he wasn't going to let me drive. I laughed in his face and said, "Oh? When are you getting your Bentley?" Truth be told, the refusal of the only gift I could afford truly hurt my feelings, but it made me realize that my first and only priority was my kids: To hell with trying to hold onto past family relationships and obligations.

The strangest thing happened at Quan's graduation. As my family was taking our many pictures, my father JoJo walked up to me and asked if he could take a picture with the boys and me. After we took our first photo ever, he asked me to make sure he would get a copy.

When I returned from my trip, my hours were cut from forty a week to ten and finally to an on call basis due to the slow summertime demand. There I was again with three college degrees and a valid teacher's certification reapplying for food stamp assistance while looking for and interviewing for teaching jobs. I was struggling to pay for daycare, and my lights were being threatened to be turned off for a $113 bill. Even though the entire house ran on electricity, I made sure not to run the bills up. I shut down everything at eight pm, and I didn't use air conditioning in the hot Houston summer in an effort to keep the bill affordable, but with no income, any amount was too much for my budget. I wasn't prepared for my job to cut my hours to zero.

I remember walking through the door holding my baby son to find my five-year-old son yelling, "Mommy, the house doesn't work." After flipping a few switches, I rushed over to my neighbor in the hope that we were having a blackout, but when I saw her watching TV, it quickly confirmed that my shit had been shut off. With teary eyes, I immediately rushed to Wal-Mart to purchase some ice to preserve my food. Then I knowingly wrote a bad check to the light company. I called my cousin who lived downtown in the hopes of going there until I could fix my situation, but instead of inviting us over, she suggested that I hook up with her neighbor's brother, who she said was receiving a hefty weekly unemployment check, to pay my overdue bill.

"Bitch, I fuck for orgasms not for little light bills," I said proudly. For the next few nights, we just slept in the back room with the window open to catch the nightly breeze, and it wasn't as miserable as I had first imagined for a Houston summer night.

Damn, I wanted to let all of the bullshit go. I wanted to say, "Fuck my sorry baby daddies. The day will come when they will have to answer for being cowards and for not even trying to help with their own kids." I have confided in my elders. I watched to church. I read the Bible to learn how to let it go and move on. But it was so hard when you thought you had let bullshit go and then had life slap you in the face with a busted water pipe in the house, or with a car making a funny noise due to overdue maintenance appointments being missed, and a daycare bill that was due whether your job had cut your hours from forty to ten and then to an on call schedule without any hours in a month. Well, I had to refer back to my Mother's Day prayer.

Please God,

Make me better not bitter. You have blessed me to come from being labeled learning disabled to multiple educational degrees. I know you didn't bless me with the drive and passion to attain my educational goals for me to rest content in the state welfare system. Lord, bless me with a career job that will enable me to provide a decent lifestyle for my family. I want to enjoy my job and still have time to be a mother to my boys.

Back Down Memory Lane

As I worked to get my household issues under control, I sent JoJo the picture that I promised. A few days later, he called to inform me that he had received it and to thank me. Shockingly, he called again that week with some small chitchat, but before I continued the conversation, I told him I wanted to go back down memory lane. He agreed.

"I just want to ask you one question: 'How could you just leave your kids and not feel guilty about not taking care of them?'"

"I did take care of y'all. Y'all got welfare, and that was all your mother wanted. Hell, I'm still paying the state twenty-five dollars a month, and y'all are grown."

I bust out laughing. All I could do was laugh, and for the first time, I understood him, my mother, and my own baby daddies. In their world the cost of a child didn't include childcare and saving for a college education.

All that time, I had been mad as hell: I wanted these people to be who I imagined they should be instead of focusing on making sure I was acting and being the best for myself. From that moment on, I tried to discard that mentality of "Why me" and started saying, "The only control I have is self-control." JoJo and I started calling each other at least once or twice a month, and he even sent me a birthday gift of a hundred bucks. Shocked again, I called and asked if he was dying.

Road to Recovery

Baby Mama Memoirs
August 2007

As the 2007-2008 school year approached, I was blessed to have several job offers. August 11th would be the big day; it was the day when all the contracted district teachers had to report to work. It was a blessing to have a job in a fucked-up economy: I was grateful to be a single mother who had a decent career and could provide for my family. It shouldn't have been this hard. All I wanted was to let go of the pain of being the sole provider for my children, so I planned to work my ass off with a smile.

I took the job with the elementary school to be involved with my own children's education and to save money by not having to put DJ in day care before and after school. That wasn't my first job choice; I wanted to work with high school students and precollege programs, but I was a single mother. With my oldest child going into kindergarten and the baby being less than a year old, I was not going to sacrifice quality time with my own child for a career title. Since teaching fed my family, I did my job with 150 percent effort. My title was elementary technology specialist, but that really meant that I was responsible for teaching my classes, training the staff on technology equipment for district/state testing, distributing & cataloging the technology inventory, creating/updating the web site, and performing basic computer maintenance.

I had come from generations of single mothers on welfare. As a child, I never saw any career fathers or mothers in my family or in the neighborhood. They said a woman couldn't teach a boy to be a man, but it was vital that I be able to teach my kids the functions and benefits of a career and an honest day's work.

My child being enrolled at my place of employment would give him firsthand experience of his mommy's career.

The first half of the school year was wonderful. I didn't miss a day, even though I was still struggling with financial issues from having to file for bankruptcy. I was grateful to be employed. I came to work an hour early each morning to get a head start on my many tasks, I worked through my lunchtime, I successfully ran one-man committees and stayed to myself by keeping my mouth shut about any campus nonsense. However, I would soon learn the baby daddies' bullshit would go hand in hand with the boss and the bullshit.

At the end of the year, I was told that "I didn't fit in" and when I questioned what about me didn't fit in. The administrator said, "It's just something about you and if you chose to return the next year, it would be a hard year for you." I told the administrator that I wasn't going anywhere until I had somewhere better to go and that I was sorry that she was going to be miserable for our eight hours together, but I would make sure to do my job and avoid her as much as possible. I filed a claim with the district Equal Employment Opportunity Commission office; and they found the claim valid. I was truly not worried about idle threats against me. However, I was scared about not being able to protect my son, because I had no family support and couldn't afford the extra expense of before and after school care to move him out of a potential negative environment. At the end of the year, a former coworker informed me about a private Christian school, and even though I would have to pay tuition for two kids, it would be better than having my child in the midst of yet another negative environment, so I enrolled him in private school for the next school year.

The Magic Show

I was really eager to relocate back to New Jersey or just anywhere in the Eastern Time Zone, so I applied for jobs in the Atlanta and Baltimore areas. I scheduled myself to attend a major job fair in Atlanta during my Spring break, but truth be told I would use the opportunity to test myself. I wanted to see if Jackson made it his business to be in the area if he knew I was coming, and I needed to know how I felt since we hadn't seen each other since the day I had left Chicago (December 26, 2005). Plus, I heard women talking about how much they loved and would always love some man who had treated them like shit. I needed to know if I was one of those women.

When he walked through the door of his sister's house and I laid eyes on him, I didn't get mad or sad, but I was a bit embarrassed that I had made such a big deal over the broken and old man standing in front of me. Jackson saw his son for the first time.

He took some pictures, and when he realized that he wasn't getting any ass from me, he hauled ass.

Once again I got the short end of the stick, because my baby daddies have the ability to brag when they talk about the women they dated or their baby mama. Not to brag, but at least they get points because I was still somewhat fit, I had a professional career, and I was cute. Damn, what good could I say about them? Nothing-- I had to keep it real. He was my "Magic Man", and like any good magician, he did his disappearing act.

The best description of both of my baby daddy scenarios is "I am their accomplishment, and they are my embarrassment".

Don't Ask Me for Shit

Baby Mama Memoirs
July 16, 2008

I didn't know what was going on with me. I should have been past all that baby daddy bullshit. However, the mere thought of not just being a single mother but knowing that those baby daddies wouldn't ever give a fuck about their own flesh and blood was scary and embarrassing. Hell yes, I was embarrassed, because I must have been one stupid bitch to have been fucking those two sorry asses. I thought it was humanly impossible for two bitches to make a baby! That's why I refer to them as dumb ass number one and dumb ass number two and to myself as the dumb-dumb who had fucked with them. Something was not connecting, and I didn't know what it was, and I was so tired of trying to figure it out. I shouldn't have been that tired; I had just turned thirty years old, and my boys were still considered babies. But the single mother shit was killing me. I wished I had a mom, a sister—hell, just any type of family support system. Even though I always sound resilient, our family consists of just my boys and I was scary shit. All my boys have is mommy right now, and I don't know if I can do it.

You see, all I ever saw growing up was baby mamas, and there had never been any talk of the pain of not being able to provide for the children or of the shame of the children's father leaving the mama and the children to struggle, but the feelings were there.

Let me make it clear, I didn't want to get back together with either of my baby daddies, nor did I want any dick from them. It just hurts to know that I've had children with men who don't care and won't provide for or even support their own blood. It was up to me to provide everything.

Let me fill you in on the details from just this past week. First, my two-year olds' father, who had only seen the kid once and was over three thousand dollars in arrears for the court-ordered child support payment of $120 per month, called and had the nerve to ask if I could send him fifty dollars for his trip to Chicago. I never pay for dick and thinking he might even desire to capitalize on the fact, I made mention of the remaining hospital balance (from when our child had to be rushed to the emergency room with a temperature of 105), and my private insurance had only covered half the bill. For him to consider me to be so stupid, made me sick.

Following that, my six-year-old was visiting his deadbeat dad for the summer and calling every day to come home. Mr. Daddy called to inform me that my son was acting out and misbehaving. "And by the way," he said, "I'm short on my rent and feel that it would be a good idea and beneficial to me to have the kid. If he stays with me, you can pay me child support since you have a good job." For the record, he'd had his own company for the past fifteen years, and he had only been ordered to pay fifty dollars a week, which he misses for a month or so and then just drops those pennies when he feels bored.

Now doesn't it seem like I was fucking some "Community Dick" bums off the street? But to be honest and fair, both of the daddies were smart and talented; they were self-proclaimed "entrepreneurs", but they haven't invested in or cared about their children, which left me asking "What the fuck? How did I get myself into this shit? How can I fix this shit?" Anyone who knew me or had even just met me could tell you that I could talk some shit; however, when that dumb shit was coming out of the mouths of my babies' daddies, I couldn't even respond anymore. I can't even believe that they had the nerve to call my cell phone to say such stupid shit.

Shutting my big mouth hurts. That was the shit that kept me up, walking the floors at night. My eyes were swollen from hours of crying, and I blamed it on my sinuses in the morning. I sometimes fought the air like Tre in *The Boys in the Hood*.

I had to get my mind right, so I started focusing on the conversation I had with my brother, before he died, about how I wanted to fix his house up. With the recent housing market crash and the numerous foreclosures in the neighborhood, his house would require a lot of renovations before it could be sold and his son could receive the profit, if any. At first the contractors that were coming in, were too expensive, so I opted to use a trusted friend's boyfriend, whose construction skills would prove appropriate to start some of the small jobs. Like most contractors, halfway through the painting job his ass tried to triple the price of the job. As I sat in the back seat of their truck trying to hold back my tears, all I could think was he wanted to rob me, so I would have to rob my dead brother. This experience made me so perturb that I decided from that point on, I would learn how to do everything by my damn self and some outsourcing with Lowes. Gutting bathrooms, tiling showers, installing floors, and changing faucet valves after work and weekends didn't leave me much time to sit around crying or complaining. My boys and I were getting it in on the home front.

Just in case you missed my fucking point, being a single mother wasn't any new shit, and getting along without family support was just like any other day in my world. However, I couldn't front. It was sad and scary to know and accept that I was in some real shit alone and that my children's biological fathers would add insult to injury by even attempting to con and steal from the hand that was feeding the children that they had left behind.

Too Busy for Bullshit

Over the summer months, I inquired about out-of-state job positions. I was trying to keep positive, but there was something about the night. During the school year, I worked and stayed involved in school programs and my kids' afterschool activities, but that summer I wasn't able to work during summer school. Therefore, I went to all kinds of free professional development training (courses on computer forensics, Microsoft office specialist training, grant writing and a fossil fuel & renewable energy conference). My school district required forty-five hours of professional development for the year, and I completed more than sixty hours before the month of August and prior to the new school year.

Hell, I was trying to figure out how I was going to pay for two college tuitions, buy another home, and just expose my kids to the world in which they had to live.

I had a folder of information from banks and books; I had met with financial consultants, and I had even tried to pick the brains of some in the finance industry. However, the stain of filing for bankruptcy and of being the sole provider of my family on a teacher's salary left me just barely making it. Damn, I missed Medicaid.

A teacher friend sent me an email about a nonprofit organization that was looking for volunteer instructors to attend training workshops and teach financial planning and career consulting to at-risk teens. The maxim of a great educator is, "If you want to learn something, you should teach it." So I was trying to kill two birds with one stone; to keep my mind too busy for baby daddy bullshit and learn more about my money. I volunteered and took away more knowledge than I could ever imagine. I knew that everything had a season and a reason. I prayed that I would learn to accept the reality of being a single mother and move on to the next season of my life.

Homesick with No Place to Call Home

I was working to get my classroom set up; I received a call from an unknown number. It was the human resource office from a Baltimore school district with a great job offer that would start immediately. I not only talked to the HR dept about the terms of their contract and salary, the Principal of this Blue Ribbon school called and said how she loved my work samples and website. We discussed how I would be used in her already award winning high school.

I was at a crossroads because I was staying in my deceased brother's house, trying to keep my word and fix it up to sell it. Now I had an opportunity to get out and start my life for my kids and me. My brother's house wasn't my home; it was left to his only son that was in college, but I was the only one fighting to save it. My brother trusted and confided in me on his death bed and I had to keep my word to him, so I declined the job offer.

It was Tuesday night, and I had to report to work on Monday morning at 7:15 a.m. Even though I was grateful and felt blessed to have a job to report to, I didn't expect to still be in Texas; nor did I want to be there. I wanted to go back to East Coast, but the truth was that, even though all of my family was there, I would still be alone. I still felt like no one understood what I was trying to do. Hell, I really didn't know how I was going to pull it off; whatever it was that I was trying to do, it would be by myself. If I did make it back, it would be on my own and I just hoped I hadn't let my chance past me by.

Facing Family

I was on the plane, returning from a twelve-day trip to New Jersey for my father's funeral. I had a window seat, and my two-year-old was in my lap, even though he had a five-hundred-dollar seat right next to me. My six-year-old was in the middle seat one row in front of me.

I was looking out the window at the clouds and the sunset, and it felt like a scene from the movies. It felt so right. I felt like I was starting to see all the things I had envisioned in my dreams become reality. There I was, sitting on a plane and typing my book up. Damn, it really felt like a daydream. I had to take seven days off work so my children and I could attend the funeral of my father. I had been a bit nervous about returning home and actually facing a lot of the family that I felt fucked me over.

Apologize for Being an Asshole

I didn't agree with a lot of the choices my mother made or some of the methods she used, but as a mother now, I understood that those were her choices to make. As I reflected on my childhood and my young adult years, I could truly admit that I was a handful to deal with sometimes, well most of the time. Realizing that, I talked to my mother and apologized for being an asshole. There were many reasons for why I had left twelve years before, for my ultimate journey to search for "something." The visit confirmed that shit hadn't changed much, but it felt good to know that I had.

Not Looking for a Husband or a Step-dad

A few weeks ago, a blast from the past felt the need to confess his undying love for me. With his heart wrenching confession, he expressed a desire to be a part of my new family life. I first asked, "Who, me? Do you remember who I am and our miserable public college breakup?" I began to run the idea through my mind of me seriously hooking up with my college ex-boyfriend; my family members and close friends all thought it was a great idea and worth a try, since this was a man who knew both the good and the evil sides of me. However, I wanted to provide for myself, and I was really not looking for the Provider Prince fantasy. You know how it goes: he meets you, the single mother, and plays with your kids, and then you're so happy that he will love them that you'll be forever indebted to him for accepting them. Fuck No.

I had gone through too many struggles to simply give a man credit for playing with my kids. As a matter of fact, that's a no-no.

I would admit that I might've been a bit jaded, and finding Prince Charming was not on my priority list right then, but he could come for a visit. He was another great college lover, and I could go for some good dick right about then. His sex had better still be great, I thought, or I will kick that ass out like I did my other ex who gave me a weak performance a few years ago.

Call Someone Who Cares!

They say trouble doesn't last always; I hope that includes baby daddy bullshit too. Chris Rock said it best when he said, "People want credit for doing what they are supposed to do." Parents are supposed to work and provide for their kids, and too many babies are taking care of the parents by providing the food via food stamps, a home via government housing programs, and health care via Medicaid. There is nothing wrong with needing and getting help. The problem comes when you build a false sense of pride based on what your child is providing via the government subsistence. The truth be told, some men-children wouldn't be in relationships if they had to provide the necessities. I assume that may be why *baby* comes first in the words *baby mama/baby daddy* to distinguish them from the parenting terms of mother/father.

If you want to know if you're dating a baby mama/baby daddy, just throw out some keys words like *insurance premiums* or *deductible* in a conversation and see if they can elaborate on them or if they even know what the hell you're talking about. Baby daddies don't want to be fathers; they just complain to the next chick about their two hundred dollars or so a month in child support and get on a working parent's fucking nerves.

I came to the conclusion that dumb asses think alike. Like clockwork, my two baby daddies bother me with their bullshit around the same time, and I guess it was their week. My blood iron level was low, my period was on, I had allergies in the Houston Spring weather—simply put, I was tired as hell and miserable. That was when the dumb asses came into play.

On Wednesday, February 25, 2009, at 9:13 p.m., I received a call from an unknown Florida number. I answered with a sleepy, "Hello?"

"Are you ready to be cooperative?" deadbeat dad number two said.

"Hello?" I said again with a tone that said "What the fuck."

"Are you ready to be cooperative?"

"What?"

"I'm just calling to let you know I got a little job and I'm going to send you some money for the baby and some for you. So how you want me to send it?"

"Hmm," I said, sighing. "Send it to the state department. That's how child support is paid."

"I'm going to send them a little something, but I'm also going to send you some money."

"Dylan has a bank account you can put some money in, if you want."

"No. I am going to send you a money order with your name on it for you."

"Whatever."

"Well, I want to speak to my son," he said.

"Around here, we have routines, schedules, and bedtimes, sir," I said.

"Well, I will call at six p.m. tomorrow"

"Yeah, yeah. Bye," I said before hanging up.

Baby Daddy Goes to Jail

My phone rang at 3:02 p.m., and when I looked down at my screen, I saw my baby daddy's mother's name. My heart began to race. I knew that something was wrong, because we only communicated when my son was down during his school breaks. I hurried to answer the phone, starting the conversation by saying, "What's going on? Is everything okay?"

His mother proceeded to tell me about my baby daddy's previous charge for having a gun on school property at an afterschool football practice for kids. She told me he thought the case would be dropped because it had been put off for more than a year, but during the trial he had broken down and had been sent to the psych ward for evaluation until his sentencing in thirty days. She said that was why our son might not hear from him.

As much shit as I talked and despite how I personally felt about him as a father, at that moment, the thought of my child's father being locked up for a possible six years shocked me.

I asked his mother how the entire event had occurred (*thinking that later I would jump in his ass about the importance of spending time with his child and not in jail*). Right then, I felt a bit sad for his mother, who has to see her son caged like an animal and who was scared about the possibility of him having to deal with the realities of prison life.

A few hours later, the shock had worn off a bit, and the anger appeared. I started reminiscing about our back-and-forth battle when the cops had gotten involved. During my baby mama days, I hadn't minded trying to knock the shit out of my child's sperm donor. The one-day that I was innocent and trying to be mature, my baby daddy had set me up and sent my ass straight to jail. I referred to that time period as the movement from the jailhouse to the schoolhouse. I wondered what he would do differently if he got out of his mess, most likely nothing. In the middle of the day on February 26th while I was at work, I got a call from an unknown Arkansas number in between classes.

"This is [*I didn't catch the name*], and I'm calling for ..."

"I wanted to call you on three-way, so that I could talk to you," deadbeat dad number one said.

"What do you want? I'm working."

"I just wanted you to know that I just talked to my lawyer. I'll be getting out on March 3rd."

"So what are you calling me for?" I asked.

"I just wanted you to know that, when I get out, I'm going to get back on my feet, handle my business, and get the child support to you."

"Who are you trying to beat in the head with bullshit? Your ass has only been in jail for thirty days, and child support is two hundred dollars a month. You can miss six months of that bullshit and that little bit of money still wouldn't put your ass in the hole. Furthermore, if you really cared about providing for your only child, your ass wouldn't be in jail for running around pulling guns on school property because of some pussy—"

"I'm not trying to hear your fucking lecture—""You called my phone, bitch," I said, "and on my phone, you will hear my mouth, so don't call me about your kiddie bullshit. Bye."

That night, the kids ate and took a bath and then we read a quick book for the evening.
At 7:58 p.m. I did the last call for the bathroom and diaper change, and at exactly eight p.m., I kissed my boys goodnight and rushed into the room to jump into bed to watch *Grey's Anatomy*.

Then the phone rang.

"Hey, what are y'all doing?" deadbeat dad number one asked.

"What? We are in bed. What do you want?"

"Oh, forgot about the time thing; you know, we only get to use the phone at certain times in here," he said. "But I wanted to talk to you, because I had a bad dream that I woke up crying and couldn't breathe."

I was thinking to myself, *What? You woke up to some dick in your mouth.*

"So what do you want?" I asked.

"I had a dream that DJ came to visit me. He was a teenager, and he walked into the house with my mom and me. He had an attitude. My mother said she wasn't going to deal with him and his attitude, because she would snatch him up. So I tried to sit down and talk to him, and I asked him why he had an attitude problem."

He had a quiver in his voice. "DJ said he was mad at me for not being there for him and for going to jail."

"I know you got your new chick on the phone, and you are trying to earn some pussy points, but you should know me by now, that I'm not going to help you fuck up some other chick's life by signing off on this bullshit you're talking," I said. "I'm tired as hell, so I'm not going to spend all night entertaining y'all asses. So with that said, let me get some shit straight for the hundredth time. You didn't have a damn dream; that's fucking reality. Let me explain what a parent is. A parent provides and protects his child and puts his child's needs before his selfish wants.

"My biggest misconception about your sorry ass was that I truly thought you were going to be a good parent, being that your ass was supposed to be so fucking sterile and you only have one damn kid. But you're selfish and immature, and you only want to play daddy when your ass is depressed, feeling guilty, or when you want to use your kid as a quick pick-me-up.

The other times are like now when you get a new bitch and are trying to earn pussy points in the "I Care about My Child" category. I can't wait until one of those weak ass sperm soldiers of yours gets some heart and produces another kid. Until then, please don't try to bother the parent that is raising and paying for our child by herself with the "I have a dream of being a daddy" bullshit."

"I'm going to show you—", he said.
"Still about *you*. You can't show me shit. Stick to your kid. He's seven and still impressionable."

"You have one minute remaining," the operator said. He had called from jail with his calling card and had his new girlfriend call me on three-way.

"Spend your last minute beating this new bitch in the head with your bullshit," I said and hung up.

I'm Fucking Done with This Father Bullshit

Baby Mama Memoirs
May 7, 2009

DJ's teacher said that he wasn't feeling well after lunch and that was why he was bearable for the rest of the day. She then informed me that, during the morning spelling test, my son had kept going into his desk between each word; she was not accusing him of cheating, but his spelling book was wide open in his desk, and she made him take the test over. We agreed that he was slipping into a phase of just not wanting to make any effort.

I was pissed because she didn't have to accuse him, but hell, we know when a seven-year-old is cheating, and I had worked with him every day on his spelling words, so I was livid. He was doing well in school with the occasional exception of kiddy stuff, but dear old daddy had just come into town to attend his cousin's wedding, and DJ had spent the weekend with him. I already knew what it was.

I fussed at this boy all the way to the car, and when I got my two-year-old situated in his car seat, I reached over to check DJ's forehead and confirmed that he was warm. I couldn't help thinking to myself, *Your ass better be sick, 'cause I was going to make you write your spelling words an extra fifteen times tonight.*

I had been down that road many times before, so I kept my over-the-counter kids' medicines up-to-date in my extra-large purse. I gave him a children's pill for fever and pain relief before we even started the ride home. When I arrived home, I ran a cool bath with green alcohol for DJ, threw some dinner together for the kids, and put them to bed early. Once they fell asleep, I planned to put DJ in the bed with me so I could monitor his temperature throughout the night.

You Can Commit to Some Coochie, But Not to Your Child

Baby Mama Memoirs
September 2009

I got word from a family member that my second baby daddy had gotten married. To top it off, he had set it up for the marriage to stay a secret so his crazy baby mama down in Texas would not find out and come and try to hurt him and his new family. But that's still not the best part of this story. Guess what? His wife was a preacher of a church, so I wondered what that made him. hmm... the con artist of the cloth.

It sure would be nice if they used some of the tithing money to pay his back child support.

Let's Keep the Man Out of Our Business

The last couple of weeks have been hectic. My stress evaluation results yielded a shocking "Very High" result, and to top off this bullshit, Jackson called and left a message for me to please call him. I waited a day or so before I returned his call just to hear him talk a whole lot of bull about having a new job and wanting to see both kids. I informed him that I had to cut it short, so he quickly requested if he could come to Houston so we could talk face-to-face.

"You can go anywhere you want at any time you want. That's not in my control. So what would we have to talk about face-to-face?"

"Dylan."
"Oh yeah? The kid you wanted dead."

"What are you talking about? I love that boy and DJ. You really need to let the past go and move on with your life. I can see you're not in the mood to talk civil about our kid."

"Oh no! Just say what the fuck you have to say, damn it."

"Well, you know I have been sending you money every time I get a check. I mean, I have been sending two hundred and even two hundred fifty dollars a month, but I can't seem to get out of arrears. I called the lady at the state department, and she said I would need to pay a lump sum, but why would I pay them a lump sum when I could just give it to you?

"Oh your arrears on one hundred twenty dollars a month for the child support order," I said laughing.

"Well, it doesn't make sense to have to pay them, when I could just give you the money. If you want a lump sum, I can give you five hundred dollars. You seem to be civil enough now that we could have an arrangement between us about this without having to go through the system."

"Wait a minute... let me get this right... So you want me to drop the court ordered child support that you refused to pay for the first three years of the child's life when you had no problem running EIC tax scams with your niece and your new wife to go on vacations and buy nice vehicles," I said.

He replied, "What are you talking about? I haven't filed taxes in years, because I know they are going to take it."

"Not filing taxes hasn't stopped you from receiving a refund check from the people you let claim your children, and you damn sure weren't thinking about your arrears then, so don't talk my head off now. Bye."

Another Mad Mother Moment

Baby Mama Memoirs
February 20, 2010

I had been planning and trying to go back to New Jersey for the past three years. I had been targeting a popular, large urban area, because I felt my skill set would be fully utilized there. Besides that, it was one of the few places I could still afford to purchase a home. Whenever an opportunity in that city presented itself, whether in the school district or in non-profit agencies, I made it my business to jump on it. I was left feeling very disappointed with the business of bullshit, but the baby mama in me didn't take no for an answer, so I kept redoing my web site and my portfolio to make sure that, when the day came, my greatness and potential would be recognizable. Well, that day may be nearing. At the end of February 2010, I will find out if I have secured a position in a renowned section of New Jersey. Guess what? I am scared. It isn't the job position or the duties that scare me; that will truly be the easy part of my life. I want to go home to be near family, as I am still alone, but when I evaluate my resources for my return home, there are none. So yeah, I am a little scared.

March 30, 2010

On March 30, my aunt Addison and I were talking about her teenage daughter, who had just had a baby, about the immaturity of both of the parents and about their new responsibility. We were trying to pinpoint why it seemed that they didn't get it and what someone could say or do to help them see the big picture about their roles as providers for their child.

"I can't relate to my little cousins' or a lot of my childhood friends' situations, because they had the baby daddies, mothers, sisters, and cousins as their support system to provide them with child care, diapers, and strollers-- they were never in a step-up survival mommy mode," I simply said. I was somewhat envious of them. However, none of those girls utilized their support systems to better their situations for themselves and their children; instead they partied, laid up with some new dick, chased their old dick, and just bullshitted. Thanks to the two man-children I had for baby daddies, I had no choice but to step up to survival mommy mode.

Ten-Year Reunion

It had been ten long years since June 9, 2000, when I had left my home state of New Jersey. The teachers' last day of school was May 31st, and I had put my oldest son on a plane to his father for the summer, the weekend before. My mother had offered to take my youngest son for a few weeks, while I started my extra summer job. All I would have to do was bring him to her home in Arkansas, but she was still in New Jersey when I decided to change my plans.

For the past three years, I had been flirting with the idea of returning home. I realized that I had left as a confused girl and that I had matured into a mother and a grown woman, who would prepare and plan if I was to return. During those three years, I had worked on obtaining my professional teaching license, searched for jobs and had numerous interviews.

I hadn't received another solid job offer since I had turned down that great Baltimore position to try and save my brother's home. I had nearly finished everything in the house when I received a letter from the bank stating that the mortgage was going to double due to a previous ARM (Adjustable Rate Mortgage) on the house. Since the house was left to my nephew, the only way I could refinance and lower the mortgage would be with his consent, and he simply told me "Let the house go to foreclosure." He even went as far as to say that he forgave me for the money; his comments suggested that I had stole the money from the house that was supposed to go to him even though the house wasn't being sold. I was so tired, I didn't argue with him, curse him out, or even try to correct his fucked up statement. I had thirty days to find an apartment, pack my shit and move my family into a cramped one bedroom. I turned my focus on finding another great position back in my home state better than the previous offer.

I had also been testing my new, grown-ass woman mode by reconnecting and interacting with the family I hadn't dealt with for the past ten years. My fear about reconnecting with my family was that the past pain would overwhelm me and take me back to my drama-filled, girlish days of confusion and bullshit. Over the last three years, I had started visiting them for a few days here and there. That grew to stays of two weeks, which was just enough to enjoy them and move on.

As I moved my school items back into my never-unpacked apartment, I simply decided I wanted to go to New Jersey, so I did. I spent the entire summer in New Jersey chilling and reconnecting with my family, and I enjoyed every minute of it. Prior to my return back South, my mother returned to Arkansas and took Dylan with her for the three weeks, while I tried to secure a job. My son's relationship with my mother mended our own "Mother-Daughter" connection. It was just my luck that the governor of NJ and the public education sector were in a major

funding battle; there were no job callbacks, so I
returned to Texas.

What a Week

Baby Mama Memoirs
August 22, 2010

It was a week before the students' return, so teachers had to report back for training and to prepare their classes. I was about 90 percent unpacked and moved into my new apartment.

Before I had left for New Jersey, I had researched housing areas and their neighboring schools, just in case I couldn't find a job up north.

I was back in Texas in a cozy two-bedroom apartment across from a park for my boys to play. The apartment also had a garage for my car and extra storage. It made the move back easier because I had a job and I would at least already have my son's school in place since I had already visited the neighborhood school and the afterschool programs. I also had my son tested for my district's Vanguard Gifted and Talented Program. Well, over the summer, I hadn't heard back from the Vanguard Coordinator, and she hadn't replied to my numerous emails. When I was able to speak to her, she informed me that my son had scored above average but that because he hadn't taken any state test in the charter school, he couldn't be admitted into the Vanguard program. However, depending on their enrollment, she said she would speak to her principal about doing an out-of-district transfer. Utilizing my usual, loquacious nature, I mentioned my previous experience working with robotics; she said that in addition to the possibility of his enrollment there might also be an afterschool job opportunity.

Just in case that didn't work out, I went to register my son in the neighborhood school I had previously checked.

To my surprise, the staff informed me that the district had been rezoned over the summer and that this was no longer my assigned school.

Now I would have to drive by two schools and out of the way to figure out how I was going to get my eight-year-old son to a school that had hours that conflicted with my work schedule, therefore forcing me to leave him home alone and to get on and off the bus unsupervised. Mind you, my son had already been unofficially kicked out of my school previously.

I was left with one option, and that was for my son to return to the charter school that lacked real guidelines, had rough kids, and did not have structured learning objectives. When I called them on Thursday morning, I was told that they didn't have my previous enrollment papers, so I told them I would be in at eleven. When I arrived, the nasty non-certified principal told me that the school had already met enrollment for the year. I was upset by her sneaky tactics and by her being unprofessional, especially at a school with such low state ratings, but I decided that if I had to beg, it would be for the best school, not the worst.

I requested my son's records and started calling the Vanguard Coordinator every hour on the hour, and when I finally got in touch with her, she took my number and promised to return my call in an hour.

The hours came and went, and I never got a return call. It was Friday, and even though I had thought I had plans A, B, and C, the choice was made for me, and I would have to enroll my son in the school that required me to train my child to become independent over the weekend. I went to enroll him during my lunch period, but I was told that I would have to come back during specific hours. When I returned, they had mistakenly put him in the first grade. They finally got it together and informed me of their required uniforms, which I would have to have before Monday. Phew... what a week.

First Day of School... Be Cool, Don't Act a Fool

Baby Mama Memoirs
August 23, 2010

The chant I sang and danced to for my students on Friday was, "It's Friday, the last day of school... Be cool, don't act a fool... Be cool, don't act a fool." Even though it was Monday, the first day of school, I was feeling cool and about to act a fool. I had my son's school squared away: the boys and I spent the weekend getting my classroom ready. Now all I had to do was begin my school year routine: up at 4:50 am, blast the *Tom Joyner Morning Show* from five until I hit the door and get to work on time.

I had left my son's new lunch bag in my truck, so I walked out the door. I saw nothing in my driveway; my truck was gone. I'd just paid the truck off four months earlier and had a new oil pan installed for a $1000 while I was in Jersey. Tears just started running from my eyes.

All I could think was *damn, why me again. What am I going to do?* I called the cops and my principal to let her know I would be a little late. As I waited for the police, I went back in to get my boys up and ready for their first day of school. While holding back tears, I decided to inform my boys that my truck had been stolen just before we walked out to wait for the bus to arrive.

As soon as I told my oldest son, he rushed to the door and said, "C'mon, Mom, we have to find your truck. It's all you have."

"Baby, it's gone," I said. "Whoever took it is not around the corner."

"But you can't give up. You have to try and find it. We need it," he said. Then he went back into the house.

A few moments later, my younger son came outside and said, "Mommy, DJ is crying."

I knew I had to save face and keep our routine going. So we all went to the bus stop so DJ could still make his first day of school. Well, we waited and waited. After about an hour and several phone calls to the school and the transportation department, a couple of parents realized that the bus wasn't coming, and once again, I was fucked.

One of the parents saw that we worked in the same school district because of the ID badge I was wearing. On her way to drop off her son, she stopped by my yard and offered to take my son with hers. I agreed, and we exchanged numbers as I placed my child in her vehicle. That may seem dangerous, but desperate times called for desperate measures. This was definitely a desperate time.

By then, it was about eight o'clock, and I was waiting for the Enterprise rental company that was less than a mile away to pick me up. Someone did pick me up; about three and a half hours later. During that time, the police informed me that my truck had been recovered. After the asshole had stolen the truck and crashed it, he had completed the job by putting it in one of the Texan bayous to make sure they did a 110 percent job of fucking my shit up. I missed the first day of school.

The next day, I got a call on my cell phone, and it was the Vanguard Coordinator informing me that a spot had opened up for my son and that he could start the next day. I really needed some good news.

Despite that ray of sunshine, as I stood there looking at my rental car a day or so later, the tears just started to fall.

I was thinking about how I had just sat down and planned to pay my thirty-eight thousand-dollar student loan off in the next five years and seven months, since I had just paid my truck off a few months earlier.

I was back at square one in humongous Texas, with no close family. I didn't even have anyone to call to take me to Enterprise to get the damn rental car. I hated being in Texas. I wanted to go home.

When I had been home that summer, I had taken my truck in for an oil change and had to leave it there for a week, because they had to order a brand new oil pan. All I did was call one of my brothers to pick me up, and I used my other brother's car until mines was fixed. That was the shit I was talking about. Living in Texas all alone was just depressing when I thought about it, but I couldn't dwell on it, because my life couldn't stop for me to pity myself.

I wiped the tears from my face and gave myself a pep talk: "Look, when has anything been handed to your ass? Spending time crying instead of planning your next move is just wasting more time. You've shed your tears, now suck it up and make some moves."

I called the person whom I had brought my two previous cars from and informed him that I would be looking for a cash car ASAP. Every day after work, my boys and I would visit the dealership's used lot to see what they had. The salesman tried to convince me that a 2002 fully loaded Camry with sixty thousand miles on it was a good deal at ten thousand dollars. Whatever, I thought. But that offer made me start looking at other options that I hadn't even considered, like visiting the new inventory part of the lot. I began researching the pros and cons of a new vehicle. My coworker and brother questioned why I kept investing in fixing up old vehicles. I replied, "Um, to avoid a car note. I'm a single mother with two mouths to feed."

I made an appointment to meet with a salesman that Friday to see what they could offer me. I had a five o'clock appointment and the high point of the evening was when my salesman returned from the finance department and told me that I was classified as a qualified buyer.

Being told that felt so good, because I had spent three or four years trying to get off of welfare for the second time and had a bankruptcy on my records. I had worked my credit score back up to qualified buyer. If you've ever had a good credit score and lost it, you know what I'm talking about, but the offer of zero percent financing was music to my ears. I opted for the rebates instead of the 0 percent, but I worked my business knowledge until about ten o'clock that night to get a 4.5 percent interest rate.

That night, I purchased my first brand new car. "I stepped down in vehicle quantity to step up in vehicle quality," I said. What sealed the deal for me was knowing that the car I had just bought would last. I would be able to make it my oldest son's first car.

September 8, 2010

I was out the door at 5:55 am. The kids were dropped off and I was in my classroom by six thirty. I was off at 3:25 pm, and the boys and I were at my second job with the afterschool program from 3:45 pm until 6 pm DJ was at the Vanguard school, but it had been a challenge to break the habits of the past couple of lazy learning environments, so we still had a couple of hours of homework and class preparation each night when we got home.

As I was working with DJ, the phone rang around 8:50 pm. It was DJ's dad who quickly said, "Hey. I'm just calling to see how he is doing." "I'm busy right now, so I'll call you back," I said and returned to DJ for another hour. I simply couldn't talk to his ass.

Why the fuck did he want a report when he wasn't trying to put any effort into raising the child? Not tonight; I had too much to do.

Four Words You Don't Say to a Single Mother You're Dating

Baby Mama Memoirs
October 28, 2010

I had been dating/fucking my new dude for over a year and I really liked our flow. We met in college and were really good friends, but when he dropped out, we lost contact. My wingman from those Jersey college days had helped us to reconnect, and on a visit to New Jersey, I swooped through Brick City to spend some time with him. Damn, he was still that bitter black man I remembered, but he was looking sexy, and he had no kids. All I knew was that he could get it.

Since he was a truck driver, he was able to arrange a trip to come and visit me in Texas. As we spoke on the phone, I informed him that I valued his friendship, but that I would be expecting some dick on his trip. With me being a busy single mom and him an on-the-road trucker, it was an ideal situation for me.

He came to town, cooked, cleaned, folded clothes, surprised me with "me time", spa days; and fucking all night: Then he was the fuck out of my face for the next two or three weeks. We had two very different personalities, but we didn't let that hinder each other's goals and lifestyles. Nevertheless, like most men, he knew how to fuck up a good thing.

Every year, I was trying to step up my "A" game and eventually get me another home and some investment property. I understood that I had to take it one step at a time; I had to first build my credit score back up to be in the 780 to 810 range. The next step was to reduce my student loans and work on building an eight-month emergency fund. More money wasn't going to just fall from the sky. My new schedule for the school year was to be up at four a.m. to get the kids to daycare and on the bus by 6:20 am. This would open up time for me to work a before-school club from 7 am to 7:40 am. I could then go and work my school hours from 7:45 am to 3:25 pm, rush and pick up my youngest son from daycare and make it to an afterschool program from 3:45 pm to 6:00 pm. I could get home by 7 pm (cook or reheat dinner, bathe, do homework and read), and have the kids in bed no later than eight thirty. This Monday through Friday schedule could stress a person out, but I had to work with what I had; Seeing my dude only three or four days a month was perfect for me and we were both clear on our purpose.

However, on his last trip, he asked if I could take him to the Caribbean section of town (that a fellow trucker had told him about). I informed that I didn't know of any such area. The request was stupid because he was from Newark, NJ so why would you be looking for culture items in the dirty south when you can buy the stuff on every corner of downtown at home.

Nonetheless, we still wasted three hours of my limited weekend time to find one little Jamaican shoebox store.

The next day as I rushed out to finish my uncompleted weekend errands, his body language made it clear that he didn't want to be bothered with my boys during the Sunday games.

When I confronted him, he simply said, "Those aren't my kids." "Hell," I quickly responded, "I know they're not your kids. I'm the one who carried those babies alone and who provides for them alone." Then I asked him to gather his shit and I told him good-bye. I knew I was going to miss him like hell, but there are four words you shouldn't say to a single mother you're dating/fucking. Mr. **"Those Aren't My Kids"**!

Open Enrollment

Baby Mama Memoirs
November 4, 2010

It was the first day for my school district's insurance open enrollment, and we had been warned that there were going to be major changes and price increases. Of course, since I lived in Texas, it was said to be because of ObamaCare, but we all knew that was just another way to fuck the working class over and blame it on having a black president.

For the four years I'd been working within that district, I'd only had its group insurance for the past two years, and it had been a costly learning experience. The first of the four years, I had kept my children on state Medicaid as long possible, and I had gone without any insurance or medical treatment in an effort to get on my feet. When the state insurance was cancelled after about six months of me working, I enrolled in a private insurance plan for about three hundred dollars a month.

When I learned about the benefits of pretax payment from joining my job's group insurance, I enrolled in it during my second year on the job. I caught hell with the damn group plan because of my lack of understanding as to how insurance worked. I couldn't wrap my little brain around how two hundred dollars was deducted from each of my checks and I still had to pay $180 to cover my two boys routine office visit. I was so happy that they always waited until payday to get sick. Deductibles were evil, and the insurance mobsters should explain that you pay the monthly premiums just to carry a damn membership card, because you still need a couple of hundred in your pocket to get some medical treatment. Well, long story short, that year I spent over seven thousand dollars out of pocket on top of my check-deducted premiums.

As a matter of fact, I just got a bill for some emergency ambulance services that insurance declined to pay for, and I would have to pay yet another $470 bill.

For my third year, I read, researched, and reviewed all types of insurance information and opted for upfront higher premiums to minimize my out-of-pocket expense. It would total more than seven thousand dollars in premiums deducted from my paycheck. I chalked up my hefty medical expenses as paying the cost to be the boss, but the new enrollment year had me scared and crying once again about I how I would be able to take care of my boys. My district hadn't just increased the premium rates of my current plan; they blew that shit out of the damn water. If I kept the plan I had for an employee and children, I would have to pay more than six hundred dollars per check, that would be more than $1200 a month just to have a fucking insurance card in my damn pocket. Motherfuckers are screaming and yelling about not wanting ObamaCare; I just wanted someone to care that a full-time teacher couldn't afford insurance for her kids, because it can't just be me or maybe it is (just me going through the medical bullshit).

Don't get it fucked up. I'm not blaming the Democrats or Republicans because my deadbeat baby daddies did not contribute to the medical costs of their children, but I wondered how the medical debate would go if healthcare benefits wasn't included in those politicians' benefits packages. Hell, cut that from the federal budget because they represent the people and the people don't get free health care... neither should they.

Last week, I filed paperwork with the state attorney's office to review and increase my youngest son's medical support and child support of a $120 a month from his father because of rising costs and the fact that his father was now employed with his state's correctional department; it was denied.

I also called my first baby daddy and told him that he needed to get a fucking job and informed him that our son was going to understand one day that his mommy was working two jobs and doing hair on weekends to provide and that his daddy was just lazy as hell.

I needed to read over some more of the insurance paperwork, because I only had until November 18th to make it right.

Searching for What You Already Have

Baby Mama Memoirs
November 11, 2010

This past Sunday I stayed in the house all day, just to attempt to catch up on some much-needed rest: to prepare for a restless week of working two and a quarter jobs, coming home to two kids, and being too tired. I returned to my Sunday tradition of watching Joel Osteen and T.D. Jakes for some weekly inspiration and free TV counseling, and the gist of the message was, "God has already given you what you need; just use it." I heard it. I discussed it. But it didn't resonate until that night.

Ever since I had been faced with being a single mother I had been searching for success, and I had started from the bottom. That was almost ten years ago, in some ways I still felt like I was in an intense search for the next big move—like a return to New Jersey or finally getting accepted to a PhD program. It seemed like, once I came to terms with the baby daddy dilemmas, I began to crave the missing factor in my career success. I was still searching and searching, trying and trying, crying and crying to the point that I didn't realize that I was not in the place I had been in ten years before. My struggles and sacrifices hadn't been without progress toward being a successful single parent.

When it's all said and done, a man or women that walks away from a child ends up leaving a part of him or herself. For whatever reason—it doesn't look like you; the other parent is crazy as hell; you didn't want it—you have the choice to walk away. If you're the child of this situation, you have the right to want to know why; but during all this, the one thing neither will ever get back, is time.

The adult who walks away will have to deal with his or her own demons, but when the fatherless child's mind begins to wander, he or she must realize that memories will be made. It's your choice whether they are going to let the memory of a missing parent make him or her a bitter or better person.

January 16, 2011, 5:00 p.m.

T.D. Jakes said, "A day of reckoning is not about what happened to you, but about how you feel about what happened to you. You can use it to become bitter, or you can become better. It's about the decision you make. If you think of yourself differently, you will live differently."

Dear God,

I asked if deadbeat dads go to heaven. I just want to thank you for giving me the clarity to understand that good memories and special moments are blessings to appreciate and can be enjoyed with or without them. We all have to deal with the hand that we were dealt, but some things result from what we did to ourselves. I still don't know, but I am no longer consumed with where the hell deadbeats go, because I'm too busy trying to make the most of my family's moments.

Too Busy for Bull,
Ms. KIA, A Mommy Making Moves

P.S. Yeah, it feels good to be home after a long, hard workweek and be too busy to be bothered by any of the simple baby daddy bullshit.

"My My"

My smile,

My style,

My choice, My child.

I wish *me* could have been *we*,

just because of the child I carried in *me*.

I used to wonder how successful *we* could be,

but you just chose to turn your back on *me*.

I gave our child your name

so he wouldn't have to wear *my* shame.

My My can only go so high,

But no longer do I wonder why,

because I'm too busy trying to see how high

My My

can fly!

Index

Dumb-Dumb Club Card

Front

Dumb-Dumb Club

Membership ID Card

Name: _____

The above named is an official card carrying member of the secret society of the "Dumb-Dumb" club.

☐ Card Carrying Clown

☐ Active & Accessible-"AA"

☐ Lifetime VIP

Back

Group Benefit Coverage

Verify Members' benefits below or call
1.555. Dumb.Luv

W — This member is running for an official office position (President, Treasure, etc.) at the Club. When you see them ALWAYS acting a fool, you just shake your head and pray the get a clue one day. The hang at the clubhouse just for fun.

AA — This member is living their lie & loving it. The have prescribed to the motto of "slow & steady wins the mate". They pay their annual dues and attend their required meetings

VIP — This member has earned the right to "PASS ON YOUR SORRY ASS" at first sight. The have paid their dues and some for a lifetime. Their attendance is no longer required.

Just Jargon

The lingo used in this book is not confined to any one culture or ethnic group. Assholes can be seen everywhere; they are from every race, creed, economic status and religious background...

Baby-mama & *Baby-daddy*	The birth parent of child/ children who is not married to the other parent and usually not in a dating relationship.
Government Gift Package -aka- "The Uncle Sam's Set-Up"	A mom and/or dad that have a baby as a means to solely provide for their basic living & household's basic necessities' such as food, medical and Section 8 housing.
Man-child	A grown ass man, technically of legal age that requires his partner/lover to fulfill his mother's role and to provide for him as if he is one of the kids in the house.
Community dick	The male version of "whore", his sex and foreplay is awesome but its too easy to get and nothing that all your girlfriends haven't already had from him.
Dumb-Dumb Club	Secret Society of current and past dumb ass lovers and a place to bury their foolish secrets.
Promise Pot	All the money collected by close family and friends for a girl to get an abortion without having to deal with the potential deadbeat daddy.
"Dick Before Chicks"	This is the unspoken rule that applies when your girl will diss your ass and/or leave you hanging for her man.
Professional Head Popper	This person is book & street smart and most likely has attained some type of degree, certification, or job status. They opt to use their street etiquette as their modus operandi in the different types of environments they enter, but above all others, their place of work. Their unprofessional attitude is the office entertainment.

Make Your Own "Happy Ever After" ...!

_____

_____

_____

_____

_____

_____

_____

_____

_____

_____

_____

_____

_____

Author's Contact

Thank You
for taking your time read the Baby Mama
Memoirs', "Dear God, Do Deadbeat Dads
Go To Heaven"..

Contact:
Ms. KIA, Author
@Ms_KIA101
FB - BabyMamaMemoirs 2.0
babymamamemoirs@gmail.com

www.ingramcontent.com/pod-product-compliance
Lightning Source LLC
Chambersburg PA
CBHW051722040426
42447CB00008B/935

9 780989 325820